BE GOOD TO YOURSELF

Thomas A. Whiting

Abingdon • Nashville

BE GOOD TO YOURSELF

Copyright © 1981 by Abingdon

Library of Congress Cataloging in Publication Data

WHITING, THOMAS A
  Be good to yourself.
  "Material for sermons on . . . the Protestant Hour for 1981."
  1. Methodist Church—Sermons. 2. Sermons, American.
I. Protestant hour (Radio program) II. Title.
BX8333.W425B4   248.4   80-27304

ISBN 0-687-02800-0

MANUFACTURED BY THE PARTHENON PRESS AT
NASHVILLE, TENNESSEE, UNITED STATES OF AMERICA

Dedicated to Helen,

*my lovely wife and companion in the ministry
whose love and constant support encourage me greatly*

PREFACE

Christianity is both personal and social. Primarily, this book is about the personal. It is addressed to people who, like Simon Peter, have been fishing in the waters of life and have found nothing. Its theme is that Christ is the Way to radiant self-discovery.

I have lived long enough with myself and with others to know how intense the search for meaning can be. We have our ups and downs, our happinesses and our heartaches. Sometimes we seem to know ourselves; at other times we don't. Life mystifies us, and left to ourselves we struggle with moods, feelings, and destructive attitudes we find hard to understand. Some of us reach the point of near despair. A few go so far as self-destruction.

I have always believed that all truth is of God and can be used to his glory. That is why I have had a lifelong interest in Christian psychotherapy. The understanding of self that has emerged from some schools of psychological inquiry has been of great benefit to Christian healers who have taken the time to study it. The chapters in this book are a personal attempt to share what I have learned in this regard for the glory of God and the helping of people.

Of course, psychology must not supplant Christ. He alone is Savior. Psychology gives us insights into who we are, the nature of our struggles, and the better life we seek. Its limitation is that it relies on human endeavor alone. It assumes that we can do what we must, a thesis disputed years ago by the great Saint Paul who cried out, "The good I wish to do I cannot; the evil I do not wish to do, I find myself doing." It is at this point that the Christian gospel, or good news, becomes so meaningful. "Thanks be to God who gives us the victory through Jesus Christ" wrote Saint Paul. Psychotherapy, then, leads us to Christ, if we let it.

The twelve chapters of this book provided the material for sermons to be broadcast on the United Methodist series of The Protestant Hour beginning in July 1981. I am honored to have been chosen for this assignment, and my prayer is that both the radio broadcasts and this book will help those who seek something in life they have not yet found.

It has been a joy to work with the producer of the United Methodist series, Dr. David Abernathy. His brilliance and talent have long amazed me, and no one knows the religious communications field better than he. His insistence on high standards of broadcasting is one of the reasons The Protestant Hour has been given the stamp of excellence through the years. It is he who puts it all together, and I am deeply grateful for what I have learned from him as we have worked together. Bill Horlock and his technical and engineering staff at the

PREFACE

Protestant Radio and TV Center in Atlanta also deserve a special thanks.

Finally, I want to acknowledge and give thanks to my secretary, Mrs. Janet Tripp, who typed this manuscript many times and who gave enthusiastic support to my ministry at First United Methodist Church in Decatur, Georgia, where I was minister when these messages were recorded for The Protestant Radio Hour.

Thomas A. Whiting

CONTENTS

1

Be Good
to Yourself

*I have often said that a person who wishes to begin a good
life should be like a man who draws a circle. Let him get the
center in the right place and keep it so, and the
circumference will be good.*

—Meister Johannes Eckhart

In the little book entitled, *How to Be Your Own Best
Friend,* the authors, Mildred Newman and Bernard
Berkowitz, ask a simple question: "Do you want to
lift yourself up or put yourself down? Are you for
yourself or against yourself?"[1]

On the surface such a question seems to be
absurd. Of course you want to lift yourself up, but
the fact is that many people do not treat themselves
as if they did. They are critical and often punish
themselves for something they may or may not have
done. Sometimes people become angry because of
unfortunate circumstances that appear to have
conspired against them. Let's think about the
question "What *does* it mean to be good to yourself?"

First of all, you are good to yourself *if you decide
what you really want in this life.* If you miss this
fundamental point, the repercussions will be felt all
down the line. If you make it at this point, you are on
your way to joyful living. Begin by asking yourself:
"What do I really want out of life?"

Obviously, there are several answers to this question. If you feel, like many people, that you have to be number one in everything you do and can never be number two or number three, you will certainly be unkind to yourself. High and impractical ambitions often produce unhealthy feelings toward yourself and toward other people.

The temptation to be restless about vocational success confronts everyone. Doctors, lawyers, teachers, office workers, and nonprofessionals all want to get to the top. Vocational success is also a major temptation for us ministers. The bigger pulpits with the big salaries and tall steeples are attractive to clergypersons. And there is a nervous rivalry within the ministerial fellowship very much like the business world. Of course we ministers must have food, clothing, and education for our children like everyone else. But the very atmosphere in which we minister can become as self-seeking as that of the business world. The result is much unrest. So we must make our careers manageable by setting realistic goals. The noted British preacher and writer Charles Kingsley advised, "Get your tools ready; God will find you work." If a minister heeds these words, he will think not so much of a bigger place to preach but of the tasks that lie at hand. He will not manipulate for a better opportunity but will so improve his capacity to minister that opportunity will seek him. That has been the story of most ministers who have been content with doing their best at all times. Such ministers know joy and peace that the more ambitious have never found.

The drive to excel others is often felt in the home. The psychological term "sibling rivalry" describes how this begins. We know that children are not alike. The first-born will always be different from the last. The child wedged in between usually grows up different from his brothers and sisters. This presents problems since it leads to both love and competition among family members.

Often this rivalry lasts a lifetime and may explode among people old enough to know better. Brothers and sisters may be jealous of each other until death. Nothing illustrates this more than a family's reactions to a will. Someone is sure to feel slighted if there are a number of heirs. Hurt feelings may never be healed. Once competition has set in, it is most difficult to deal with. We should watch over our attitudes toward members of our own families seeking to develop feelings of love and appreciation rather than of crippling competition.

In determining what we want in life, we will have to come to terms with the meaning of happiness. Many people see this as life's most important goal. Yet persons who deliberately set out to be happy will never attain their goal. When deliberately sought, happiness escapes us. It is like quicksilver in our hands—the more we pursue it the more it eludes us, though we never give up the quest. In the well-known movie *The Wizard of Oz*, Judy Garland sang a beautiful song, "Somewhere over the rainbow bluebirds sing . . ." The song ends its lament with, "Birds fly over the rainbow, why, then, oh why can't I?" Surely we all identify with Judy. We want happiness for ourselves, and we pursue it avidly. But life is so made up that we can't have our cake and eat it too. We must come to terms with this reality and discover that the supreme goal of life lies elsewhere.

If our goal cannot be happiness, what is it? Simply this: to live with purpose and meaning. The logotherapist Victor Frankl taught that if you can find meaning in what you do, anything is tolerable—even pain and death. If you do not find meaning, life at any level becomes a drudge. You will be good to yourself if you keep this goal in your awareness and pursue it as your main objective. Strangely enough, you will discover that the happiness which you once sought through direct assault comes in unnoticed through one of the windows of your spirit. But be careful! Do not turn to look at it and caress it! The minute you stroke it, it is gone! You will find happiness more readily when you don't care about finding it but do care mightily about doing some worthwhile thing with your life. Then, and only then, will happiness slip in unobserved to bless you.

Another point to remember is that all of us have to adjust to change. You are good to yourself *if you accept that change will come into your life, if you expect it and adapt yourself to it.* It is impossible to live without undergoing change. Our bodies are constantly changing. Our minds are subject to this also. We discover that we must constantly adjust to the winds that blow from one direction and then another. Some recent studies indicate that if change is thrust upon a person too rapidly and in too many forms, it can have tragic results. I hope this will not happen to you and that you would have time to make adjustments to change. But whether swift or slow, change we must.

How can we handle change daily? One way is to *recognize that life is not a goal but a process.* Carl Rogers, a noted psychologist, has given us this idea in his "Process Psychology." He believes that life is not static but is movement. He feels that to become "me" I must express my feelings fully and be open every moment to the things which occur within me. My feelings will be negative and positive, and I must discern what I'm feeling and accept responsibility for the level on which I will operate as a person.

Dr. Rogers urges us to trust the organism of our being. On the other hand, Evelyn Underhill warns us that absolute self-expression will bring complete chaos. We need to be responsible for our changing feelings and their expression. To recognize that life is constant movement and not static finality is to put one's self in the position to welcome change.

But there is another side to this matter. Alvin Toffler, who authored *Future Shock,* suggests that there are people who love change. They want something new all the time—new wife, new husband, new automobile, new clothes, new movies, new food, and so on. They seem totally unhappy with anything that is old. But Toffler points out that as you look deeper into their lives, you discover that there are some stable qualities. If this were not so, survival would be impossible.[2]

It seems to me that stability *is* the crucial point. We

are responsible for ourselves in the midst of the changes which surround us, and to be truly responsible, we must look for those beliefs and actions which keep us steady. We begin dealing with change by asking ourselves What is basic? What things do I want to build my life on? Let these be the lenses through which you see and accept the future.

Another way you can be good to yourself *is to love yourself in the right way.* Love can be misdirected. At times you hear it said of a person that he does not love anybody but himself. Is this really true? I doubt it. I'm not even sure that this can be called love. Such a person is simply centered upon himself. The Greeks had a word for this which sprang from the legend of Narcissus. Narcissus was the name of a young man who was forced by a river nymph to look at his own reflection in a pool of water. The youth fell in love with himself to such a degree that he would not eat or drink. Ultimately he died. Thus was born one of the better-known words of our psychological vocabulary, "narcissism," which means abnormal attention given to one's self. But it is not to be confused with loving one's self.

Most of us would not go so far as Narcissus, but we do like to give attention to ourselves. It is amusing to visit a shopping center where there are many mirrors and watch people pause to look at themselves as they walk by. Most of us have caught ourselves doing this. It is not uncommon to see people arranging hair, straightening neckties, or adjusting clothing. This is quite normal, and we call it pride in appearance. But it is quite another thing to look at one's self and say, "You awful thing. I despise you!" It is far better to be up on ourselves than down on ourselves unless a critical review is justified and from it there can emerge a better person.

But, such self-attention is not true love. To love yourself in the right way means that first of all you accept the uniqueness of your own creation. There is no other human being like you. You bear the same name God ascribed to himself in the Old Testament: "I am that I am." Note how intensively personal this is. Many meditation cults help individuals to feel their personal identity and self-worth. But the most important thing is to sense that you are a unique person because in your creation you were loved by God. This means that you should accept yourself for who you are. That's a wonderful beginning toward the discovery of the right kind of love.

Then you have to ask yourself, "What was intended in my creation?" One answer would be that you should follow the directions that have been given for your use. It's like the parents who were trying to put together a Christmas toy for their child. The toy wouldn't fit together properly. One of the parents spotted a sticker on one of the pieces that read, "If all else fails, read the directions!" Well, why not read them first? And why not apply them to our personal quest? We know who we are and for what we were intended by paying attention to these directions.

Where do the directions come from? Some

knowledge comes by ventilation of our feelings, by sensing what is inside us. But we do not gain complete knowledge of ourselves in this fashion. Much more comes to us from the outside, from the compiled experience of thousands of years of living, which is ours to contemplate and profit from. Perhaps this is why Oliver Cromwell said to a tutor who taught his son, "I would have him know a little history."

Part of history—a very important part—is the story of Jesus and his love. Here is where psychotherapy becomes Christian. We discover the directions for our use in a man, a very special one, a historical figure, Jesus, the Son of God. When he came into the world he spoke concerning God and revealed to us the true nature of life. He called God's directions for our lives "The Way." This Way also meant the coming of forgiving love for everyone since all had failed to heed this Way. When understood, this act of love adds greatly to our sense of self-worth. Just to know that we are loved individually, in spite of our sins, by him who created the world is a saving truth. It is impossible to estimate how many people have been saved from feelings of inferiority or have been lifted from their loneliness by becoming aware that the wonderful God Jesus talked about really does love them—even if no one else does. When a person senses this, he knows that he counts. He is somebody to God! And, he is somebody to himself!

Once we accept God's love and begin to live in it, we discover that it has a certain magic. We find ourselves being open in our love for others, a necessary step toward true fulfillment. There is also a love for all of life—a glass of cold milk, a walk in the late afternoon holding the hand of a loved one, the song of the birds in the morning, the colors of autumn, the laughter of children. All of life is made beautiful by love!

Also, when we love others, or lose ourselves in the service of Christ, it brings the richest earthly rewards. It is an unsolved mystery as to why life should be so fulfilling when we love, but it is true nevertheless. We cannot understand it, but we can experience it. We discover that love carries its own blessing with it. There is something built into its nature like the sweetness of an apple or the fragrance of a flower. Love frees us from crippling self-consciousness since it takes us away from thoughts of self. Many of us battle with self-consciousness all of our lives but discover that we are freest from it when we have invested our lives in loving others.

One man who helped me learn this was Richard Niebuhr, my professor of Christian ethics at Yale. In a letter which I shall always treasure, he shared with me the agony of self-consciousness he sometimes felt as he stood in the pulpit to preach. This condition had not left him as he grew older. "But," said he, "it always leaves me when I begin to think of someone in need sitting there on one of the pews whom I might be able to help." I heard him preach often and his sermons were powerful. There was no hint of self-consciousness. He escaped preoccupation with self through service and love.

Love also makes us brave. Cowardice springs from caring too much about what will happen to us. "Perfect love casts out fear." When our attention is away from self and placed on God and others, we are not as concerned about what others might do to us or what the future holds.

We need not miss out on the wonderful thing life can be. We can leave destructive attitudes and acts behind and give ourselves to something better. In so doing, we will be good to those selves which God in his goodness gave to us.

2

Big Worries
and God's Care

*As God looks upon us he sees the inherent ability, the hidden
beauty, the unused power of spirit in each of us.*
                                                —Muriel Lester

The medical term "symptom" is defined in a
dictionary as "an organic or functional condition
indicating the presence of disease." In plain
language this means that if you have a pain in your
right side, it could indicate the inflammation of your
appendix. If the pain is in your stomach, it could
mean an ulcer.

If we apply this to our emotional problems, we
sense right off that there are certain symptoms, such
as chronic worry or anxiety, which indicate some
deeper psychological trouble. Just as we know the
implications of physical symptoms, we also know
that painful anxiety is a cry for better emotional
health.

Like other moods we have, however, anxiety has
its place. Perhaps you are familiar with the
announcement made each evening by some TV
stations just before the 11 o'clock news. A voice
comes on saying, "It's 11 o'clock; do you know
where your children are?" The assumption is that all
of us should know the wherabouts of our children.

Some parents will not be anxious since their children have agreed to be home by a certain hour. But if the time is 3 o'clock in the morning and there was no previous agreement concerning curfew, parents will become concerned—and, they should. In this situation worry is a very good thing. You can worry yourself sick about your health, business, or future, and this is harmful, but if you don't show a normal amount of concern about these matters you are certain to run into trouble. So, one good word of advice to all of us would be, "Be anxious—but within normal limits!" A normal, emotionally healthy person will show anxiety, but only under proper conditions.

There is also a crippling, chronic anxiety that is altogether debilitating, and this is what we must learn to manage. Such anxiety is experienced as the feeling of being trapped. We are possessed by a negative, unsure, often hysterical or panicky feeling about ourselves. Accompanying it is fearfulness. We agonize over decisions and generally live a tensed up life. If this is your problem, you know that you do not want to remain in this painful condition. Yet, if you are like most people, you find it difficult to extricate yourself from it.

What can be done? First of all, there is need for some understanding of the situation. Seek out, as best you can, the cause or causes for your anxiety. Ask, "Do these causes lie within those things that concern me or do they lie within me?" The correct answer to this question is most important.

Years ago I wrote Dr. Harry Emerson Fosdick about some problems of belief I was wrestling with in the years following my graduation from seminary. Always prompt to answer his correspondence, he replied by stating that he was not quite sure whether my problem was in me and therefore psychological, or intellectual and therefore theological. His response got me thinking, and soon I had managed my way through the problem. In this instance, the cause of my unbelief seemed to be me and my lack of confidence in assuming my own theological stance.

One good rule of thumb is to assume that the solution to anxiety is related to what is happening on the inside of you rather than on the outside. There are exceptions, but you have probably noticed that when two people face the same problem one will often manage it far better than the other. The difference is on the inside. So turn inward to ask what has caused you to feel this way. Hopefully, a little introspection will produce some clues.

In trying to understand your problem further, your efforts need to move in two directions. If for no obvious reason you are anxious all the time about yourself and people to whom you relate, you might profit by going back into your life history. Again this is an inside job—right inside your head. Step back into your personal history for a while and look around. What do you see? One of the awarenesses which may come to you is that you got your fearful attitudes from your parents or from your life situation. Some of them might have been produced by the era in which you grew up. There are anxieties associated with the great economic depression and others with the atomic age. If most of what you remember about your past is more depressing than uplifting, then you have good cause to suspect it of producing within you some of your anxiety. There is no doubt that we can learn anxiety from our parents just as we can learn positive, outgoing attitudes from them. If you have been so fortunate as to receive a healthy approach toward life from your parents, be grateful! But if something back there has caused you to be negative and withdrawn and therefore anxious, you must unlearn these attitudes in order to be positive and productive in your living.

At this point let me lift a flag of warning. Don't let what you remember about your past cause unforgiven bitterness toward your parents or their life-style, or anything else which has marked your past. Bitterness can become a problem which compounds the other one, thereby increasing your anxiety all the more.

What is essential is a willingness to forgive. We must forgive the past, forgive our parents and the mistakes they may have inadvertently made in our rearing. To ease this process it helps to know that someone probably taught them the debilitating attitudes which they passed on to us. Thus they cannot be completely blamed. But whether this is true or not, it is important to say, "I forgive and release my past!" That is a good start toward overcoming anxiety.

It helps also to see that we may be in the same predicament as our parents! As anxious persons, we may be teaching others to perform in the same way. Thus we are in need of forgiveness from them. This helps us understand that marvelous petition which is found in the Lord's prayer, "Forgive us our trespasses as we forgive those who trespass against us." Because we are in need of understanding and forgiveness for our mistakes, we must be forgiving of others who have made them against us. Forgiveness, either of yourself or of others, is a cleansing process. It lances the wound and removes the poison. It gets rid of the bitterness and remorse which may increase your anxious state.

Forgiveness can help you overcome what may be your greatest lack—being loved as a child. This, too, may have been the lot of your parents, who may have failed to receive the love which they were due. You are more likely to find this love through an understanding and forgiving spirit than through an unforgiving one that leaves you morose and unloving.

In addition to looking back into past experiences, you also need to look ahead. What is it out there that you really want? Is it realistic or impossible? Our goals must be attainable, and if they are not, we become anxious. Take marriage, for example. One reason that couples fail in this union is that they expect the impossible of it. They make unrealistic performance demands of each other. Of course this can't work.

On this point, even the marriage ritual adds to the pressure! There is a prayer at the close of the marriage service which has the officiant praying that the couple might live in "perfect love." But what relationship is perfect? Can anyone succeed under such an impossible demand? Perfection is for God and the angels alone! We are human creatures, and we must make a marriage out of what we have. Thus, if you are a married person and are concerned about your marriage, don't make the mistake of expecting perfection from your mate in feelings of love, sexual performance, disposition, or the like. Your love temperature isn't going to be 98.6 degrees always, so don't expect it. Keep love alive as best you can, of course, not taking your mate for granted, but recognize that your best is less than perfect.

This same anxiety might be present in your social relations, your job performance, or the pursuit of happiness. Here again your demands have to be realistic. If you expect more out of yourself than you can produce, then you are a candidate for misery. Let me ask you this: Are you guilty of what could be called the pinnacle syndrome? Do you have to be first in everything? If so, you will be chronically anxious! Every person of any means, talent, or beauty will be a threat to you. This is why there is so much neurosis in Hollywood. All of the movie stars there love the limelight, and it is difficult for any one of them to take second place.

The cure for this syndrome is self-acceptance coupled with wholesome, realistic ambition. Be the best *you* can be. If that takes you to the top, be grateful. But second or third, when it is your best, should be accepted. This doesn't mean that you throw in the towel concerning your performance level; it does mean that you bring your talents and the opportunities you choose into a wholesome balance. You will perform better at the level commensurate with your abilities than you will when you are over your head.

This means an acceptance of your limitations. Maxwell Maltz, the plastic surgeon turned psychological counselor to thousands, has written in one of his books, "To live successfully, realize that you are capable of making a mistake." But Dr. Maltz would also urge that you do your best. As a matter of fact, he tells us that when he was a student at Columbia University hoping to enter medical school, he failed organic chemistry. After that he thought his plans to be a doctor might be over. But he decided to go to summer school and take organic chemistry again. This time he passed with flying colors. So I am not advocating low aim when one is capable of high performance. That is taking the easy way out. It will take judgment to know what is realistic, but each of us, while displaying courage and ambition, will need to find his or her performance level and accept it.

Actually, we must accept life with both its possibilities and limitations. It may seem a rather somber thought, but you must accept the fact that you live and that at some point you will die. According to the existentialist philosophers, death is the cause of our greatest anxiety. They say we are always aware of death, although we seek to shun the thought as much as possible.

One of the results of our preoccupation with death is that we may be driven toward hypochondria. We may be so concerned about staying alive that any slight physical discomfort makes us anxious. We may learn this from our parents and others. Consider the delightful little story about a family in which the flu made its rounds during the winter season. Medications were taken by all and the thermometer passed from mouth to mouth. When they were all recovering, the little four-year-old boy indicated at the close of his evening prayer that he had picked up the family concern about health when he prayed, ". . . and, dear Lord, give us all normal temperatures!" It is certainly possible to have the seeds of hypochondria sown in us at a very early age, simply because we are concerned about staying alive. It is good advice, therefore, to be attentive to our health, but not overly so.

Another one of life's realities is that conditions surrounding our lives do not remain the same. This tends to make us anxious. C. S. Lewis once wrote a letter to woman who had written him about a move she was having to make in her life. She feared it and had written for his advice. In his reply he told her that he shared her feelings. He liked the same old horizons, the same garden, the same smells and sounds, always there, changeless. As he put it, "The old wine is to me always better." But having written this he then went on to indicate the futility of this position: "We must 'sit light' not only to life itself but to all its phases."[1] So we must. We have to accept this universe and the limits of our creation. We are here for a while only. Things never remain the same. But, this need not strike fear in our hearts. Indeed, it should provide an opportunity for greater courage which God will surely give us.

What helps most in all of this is to place our lives within God's care. Frankly I do not know of any other way to overcome chronic worry. Self-help achieves a degree of peace, but it does not strike at the deepest roots of the problem. Only faith in God can achieve this. About such a faith the apostle Paul wrote unforgettable words to his Philippian friends: "Have no anxiety about anything, but in everything by prayer and supplication with thanksgiving let your requests be made known to God. And the peace of God, which passes all understanding, will keep your hearts and your minds in Christ Jesus" (Phil. 4:6-7). I have quoted these words to myself and others hundreds of times, and I know that they work. They link us to our God whose supply of power and love is inexhaustible.

So, if you are an anxious, nervous person, it is here that you can become a conqueror instead of a victim. Remember how Kagawa, the great Japanese Christian leader, put it? As a young person and an illegitimate child, he was miserable and ridden with anxiety. Then he met a missionary who told him about Christ. The missionary read to him the

Sermon on the Mount. One day Kagawa accepted and felt God's love. He heard God saying to him, "I will make you one of my flowers. . . . There is no need for you to be anxious; for I am with you. Just grow, stretch out your roots and grow!"[2] That changed everything. What was available to Kagawa is surely open to you. You need only believe and practice such faith. Begin now to believe and grow.

3

You and
Your Feelings

A man needs to feel something in this slippery world that holds.

—Herman Melville

A minister was asked by a friend one day, "What is the greatest problem you face in your ministry?" His answer was, "Myself!" This man was not stretching the truth. He was putting his finger on the most difficult task we have, managing ourselves.

A human being is a complicated creation, so enigmatic that he is often a mystery to himself. He finds himself to be a person of conflicting attitudes and feelings, some of which reward him, while others bring only a sense of defeat. Some bring him quite close to others, but some seem to have the opposite effect.

Such a variety of feelings is portrayed in the *Peanuts* comic strip characters of Charles Schulz. The chief character, Charlie Brown, is a born loser. He is the epitome of negative feelings. Nothing is ever right. It is Charlie Brown who says, "When my ship comes in I will probably be at the airport!" Then there is Linus who has to have his security blanket. The feeling of having to have something to depend on is well known to each of us. And Lucy, how can she be described? She is a holy terror.

31

Unhappy herself, she will not allow anyone else to be happy. Then there is the bright spirit we know as Snoopy, the dog.

There are other feelings, of course, and all have a mysterious quality about them. Often they are unpredictable. They just appear. One example concerns a girl who has been dating a young man for a very long time, a fine fellow in every way. With her reason she concludes that he is just the kind of person with whom she would like to fall in love, but try as she may the feeling of love will not come. This troubles her no end, and she wonders if it will ever work out. Then one day when she least expects it, she sees him in a different light, in a new set of circumstances. Maybe he is wearing something different. At any rate, things have changed, and suddenly and mysteriously it happens. She feels love for him.

Such a happening is a fortunate thing, but it can work in the opposite direction also. A woman loves her husband as he loves her. She works in an office where there are number of attractive men. One day she discovers to her dismay that she is developing an infatuation for a man who is also married. He responds to her in the same way. Reason says to both of them that such feelings cannot be productive and may indeed be tragic, but the feelings are strong. In most instances people turn these feelings off, but occasionally there are those who give in to them, and the results can be damaging to both families.

The management of how we feel becomes very important to the success of our daily living. We must learn to recognize feelings for what they are, encourage those that give us greatest joy and the most rapport with fellow human beings, and manage those which affect us adversely.

In doing this there are some guidelines to help us. First of all, *feelings must be looked at as honestly as possible by the one who feels them.* There must be frankness and openness which allows you to examine what hurts you. Begin searching for some explanation as to why you feel as you do. You may find some answer on your own, or you may recognize a need for professional help.

Then, accept your feelings as being a part of yourself. They are a part of you, and you will never get very far by rejecting them as being unreal. Don't be reluctant to *feel* your feelings. If you run from them, battle them, or repress them, they will linger to give you much mental and emotional distress. Psychiatrists urge us to ventilate our feelings. Let a little light in on them and then have courage to accept what you see. Whatever that feeling might be—depression, loneliness, sexual temptation, irritation, hot temper, hostility, or something else—you must recognize it as being a part of you. That's the only way you can work through it.

It is also a good thing to talk to someone about your feelings, a trusted friend or a counselor. Do not talk to everyone! There is an old adage which says, "Show your wounds only to a healer." You will not want to talk to everyone since this might confuse you. Also, it is a good way to lose friends! Lasting friendships cannot be established when one person is asking for help from the other all the time. But, it is good to discuss your problems with someone else. One reason for this is that thinking about it by yourself has its limitations. You are already involved emotionally, which makes it difficult to put things in true perspective. A friend whom you trust or a professional counselor will not suffer from this limitation and can see things more objectively.

Another aid which you may employ is to *write things down*. If you cannot talk to another person or cannot afford a professional counselor, talk to your notebook with pencil or pen. A typewriter is just as good. It might help to write a letter to someone about a feeling you have, even if the letter never gets mailed. Thousands of such letters are written daily and serve to clarify the issue at hand. Even the destruction of such letters is not without some significance. It indicates the end of time given to serious analysis of one's problem. It may also indicate that an understanding and a solution have been reached.

In dealing with your feelings *you ought not brood over them too long at a time*. Alternate between introspection and activity. Brooding for long periods is liable to magnify your problem out of all proportion to its real size and can cause you to panic. So, do not stay with your problem constantly. Don't get away in some corner to stroke your fears, engage in too much self-pity, or too much introspection. The great logotherapist, Victor Frankl, calls this preoccupation with self "hyper reflection," and it is a bothersome introspective state you want to avoid.

Go out into the world and become busy for a while, returning later to a quiet place to look again at your feelings. When you return you will be able to see yourself better.

It might be helpful also to *check with your physician for physical causes which may underlie your problem.* A person who is rundown physically is a fit subject for feelings of depression and unexplained irritability. Emotional hangups can produce fatigue, of course, but so can physical illness. And keep in mind that everybody over forty has something physically wrong! Our physical problems may be large or small, but they are there.

Sometimes, as in the case of menopause, emotions and physical changes combine to affect the feelings. Some women seem not to be affected by these changes, while others find them very painful. Your doctor can help you understand yourself when this occurs whether you are a woman or man. Don't forget that while women seem to feel the effects of menopause more than men, males go through life changes, too. It is a wise man who knows this and learns to deal with it. He should not hesitate to discuss it with his doctor.

Next, let me suggest that you *accept what can't be changed.* In the Bible there is a verse which asks, "Can the Ethiopian change his skin or the leopard his spots?" (Jer. 13:23). Of course not. This means that there are some things about yourself which you can change very little. There are some things which are just "given." If you are robust in body, have healthy nerves, are an outgoing person, and don't have any neurotic hangups, then rejoice, my friend, rejoice! You are a fortunate person, and your problems may lie at some other point. But if you are frail of body, nervous in temperament, and have a tendency toward emotional suffering, you must rejoice, too, because that's what you've got! You have to start there. A little careful study of the history of human beings will indicate to you that this is not all bad. As a matter of fact, some of our most creative people have been so disposed. The important thing is to be aware of your basic makeup and to accept that as a starting point.

This simple bit of wisdom must be used as you relate to your past. There isn't one thing you can do to change the happenings of yesterday. There is nothing which you can do to undo your background, whatever it is. You can know and benefit from all of these things, but you cannot change them. Many times individuals will say to a counselor, "I had an unhappy childhood. My parents mishandled me. My home life was not enjoyable. It left me insecure." The counselor will listen to this and feel sympathetic because it is true of many of us. But then he will have to say, "But you really can't change all of that can you?" Some accept the fact that they can't, but some keep trying and theirs is always an attempt to move an immovable object. There are times when a counselor will suggest to such persons, "You are blaming your parents for your unhappy lot, but have you ever stopped to think that others had some effect on them?" Such a realization might make it easier to accept the facts of one's past and, what is more important, to forgive them. That is a must if you are to have healthy feelings.

Next, move on to see that you should *change what can be changed*—which is a lot. You do not have to give in to destructive feelings like depression, hate, jealousy, or irritability. You admit them and then deal with them as calmly as you can. "But," you say, "how is this to be done?" Well, you can make use of your own resources of reason and will. You can reject (not repress!) the thoughts that cause unproductive feelings and invite the thoughts which produce their opposite. The idea is simply not to entertain negative thoughts. This is what Jesus meant when he said, "If your right eye causes you to sin, pluck it out and throw it away. . . . If your right hand causes you to sin, cut it off" (Matt. 5:29, 30). By this Jesus did not mean that one should literally pluck out one's eye or cut off one's right hand. He did mean that if something comes into your life by eye or hand that is destructive to your well-being, you should cut it off—stop immediately! That is certainly good advice.

One contemporary author urges us to undertake what he calls, "Don't think."[1] By this he means that we are simply to refuse to think at all, to practice emptying our minds of everything during certain measured periods. By doing this, he says, the negative thoughts will not be entertained and the positive ones will come trooping in. There might be something to this, though it is difficult to pull off. I prefer to say, DO THINK! Not only don't think about the negative, but do think about the positive which can produce good feelings within you. Think of something good about yourself, about God, about life and the opportunities it still gives you.

Here you will begin the formation of new habits of thought to take the place of old ones, and it will not be easy. It is never easy for a person who has lived with negative thoughts all of his life suddenly to live positively. But persistence wins. You *can* reject these negative thoughts as they come to you. You *can* change old habits and begin new ones. Remember, "As a man thinks in his heart, so is he!" Let those thoughts be positive!

To help you achieve this, *make use of prayer. Be careful, however, to pray positively.* If when you pray to God you simply tell him how bad things are and keep telling him this over and over again, you will not get much help. The reason is that you are still absorbed in your problem and have no attention left for the source of your help. Whatever gets your attention gets you, and if your depression or some other problem looms larger in your mind and has a greater grip on you than the presence of the Heavenly Father, you get nowhere. This can happen even to those who pray most earnestly.

God has made you a great promise. In the words of Jesus it is, "Blessed are those who mourn, for they shall be comforted!" That's the way it is stated in the Sermon on the Mount, but in order for it to become yours you must change the tense. Take it out of the future tense and bring it into the present. You might paraphrase it like this: "Blessed am I who mourn, for I am being comforted right now, in this moment, by my Heavenly Father!" This is claiming the promise. It is appropriating the power and loving presence of God. It is concentrating on the remedy and not only the problem. It is positive prayer that will produce results if faithfully continued.

One day a chaplain on any army base walked into a chapel and unknowingly disturbed a young GI who was in prayer. The young man sat with his head on his hands which were folded and placed on the top of the pew in front of him. When the chaplain realized he had interrupted the soldier, he walked toward the young man with some embarrassment. He apologized and asked, "Can I be of any help to you?" The young man replied, "No thanks, I am being helped." That's the way prayer should work—not always seeking, but receiving through faith.

One reason we find it difficult to pray positively is that too often we are comfortable with our feelings of frustration. They hurt us, but still we do not want to let them go. At times, we must be reduced to most extreme conditions before turning them loose. Most of us find our sufferings bearable because they are ours. We are familiar with them, and if we must choose between the familiar and the unfamiliar, we are tempted to stay as we are. We have a difficult time breaking away from the feelings that distress us but bring us some comfort in a twisted sense. Yet we know that if we are ever to be our happy selves, we must make this move. It is to this that Jesus calls us. During his earthly ministry he talked to those who were crippled in body and spirit and encouraged them to step forth and be made whole. He called them to a positive, hopeful life. Since he is the universal Christ, timeless in his message and ministry, that offer is for you and me now.

We sense that a great deal of healing is being offered us today. Much of it, however, is on the human level alone. Many of the teachings we are urged to accept are described as mind control and self-hypnosis. These are not new. They have been around for many generations. The content is the same; only the name has changed. However, they are new to those who have come freshly to this generation. Some of these teachings have merit as far as they go, but because they ignore or minimize divine help, they do not relate to the ultimate reality about which we are concerned. Thus, they deny their followers meaning for the totality of living.

Christianity is different. It urges you to use your mind and best understanding in getting at your problems because God gave them to you for this purpose. It is reason that also motivates you to seek the counsel of a trained professional. Here we express appreciation for the members of the healing profession who have the difficult task of trying to help people ferret from their tormented spirits those things that are hurting them inside and destroying their relationships with others. They do a good job, but in all too many instances healing takes place only on the human level.

Christianity teaches us that healing also comes from life with God. As we live in him, in his Son, in his Spirit, we find strength becoming ours. We find the courage we need to break from our captive fears. We find the resolve to handle our feelings and not give in to them. We sense that we are supported by a great and eternal God who is stronger than all we will ever have to face. When this realization sweeps over us, we know that we can emerge from our struggles stronger and better. We then see how our feelings can be managed and made to work for us.

4

Your Personal
Health and Peace

"I'm gonna open another window and let the sun shine in!"
—a song sung by Ken Medema

There is a restlessness about human nature which reveals itself at every hand. After World War II, the editors of *Look* magazine, sensing something was wrong with the American people, sent their editors and writers to every section of this nation in an effort to feel the nation's pulse. When the research was over, a series of articles appeared, indicating that few Americans felt any joy. Such a conclusion seemed all the more astounding since America was in the midst of a postwar boom. This absence of joy and inner satisfaction still characterizes our people today. Thousands of people ask themselves, "Why aren't I satisfied?"

I would like to look at this problem of dissatisfaction with you through the eyes of two groups of people: first, non-Christians, and then those who call themselves Christians. Oddly enough both feel dissatisfied, though there is a difference between the two as we shall see.

The laments of the unbelieving man or woman are the inevitable result of a life lived away from God. Christian theology has always taught this, and the effects of Godless living are more pronounced today. It is not what a person lacks in material things or his failure in some vocational choice that provides the root cause of his dissatisfaction. It is the simple fact that God goes unaccepted and unrecognized in his life.

When a person lives unmindful of spiritual truths and the presence of God, he structures his life at the level of materialism. Here he is sure to find no lasting satisfaction. As Ecclesiastes, the Old Testament preacher put it, "The eye is not satisfied with seeing, nor the ear filled with hearing" (1:8). This means that even if we have all we want, we do not want what we have. Life can be filled with any number of things and events but still go lacking. This says something to us about the peril of solving our problems on economic or social levels alone. Attempts in these directions will do a great deal of good, but unless the divine-human relationship is established, they will never bring lasting satisfaction to individuals and to societies. Christian belief has always known that when a man turns away from God, he is like a fish out of water or a bird out of the air. Man is out of his natural habitat when he rejects the one who created him and refuses to have fellowship with him.

Because this God relationship goes unmet, there is a terrible longing and restlessness in man's life which often results in cynicism and despair. Playwrights of our time have been quick to sense this. They are honest enough to recognize the folly which lies in human striving apart from some deeper relationship. In his drama *The Misfits*,

Arthur Miller depicts pathetic human creatures who seek meaningful life apart from God. What is odd in Arthur Miller's script is that God seems to be in the wings but is never called on stage. *The Misfits* is a tender story about a group of cowboys and a divorcee who meet in what seems to be Reno, Nevada. The cowboys participate in a rodeo from which they hope to make some money. Rosalyn is there seeking some meaning for her unfulfilled life. The cowboys manage to win a little money. With Rosalyn they visit a night spot where suddenly from the crowd there emerges a little religious woman who parrots phrases about damnation and salvation. In her hand she holds a tambourine, seeking an offering from those who are visiting the place. Rosalyn, moved by the woman, takes one handful of money after another from the winnings and places it in the tambourine. As she looks at the little woman there is longing in her eyes. But suddenly it all ends. Exit God! God seems to be there as a determining factor, but suddenly the playwright makes a decision to keep him in the wings. Later in the story this rather helpless and beautiful young woman, now involved in an illicit love affair, stands outside a dilapidated ranch home and looks into the darkness of night to cry one word, "Help!" At the end of the story, after an experience of hunting and corralling wild mustangs that will be sold to meatpackers, Rosalyn and her lover ride off the range. It is dark and she asks, "How do you find your way home in the dark?" Looking through the windshield of their old car, her lover replies, "See that star? Underneath it is a highway and it will take us home!" The only trouble is that it wouldn't! It is evident that the playwright does not believe in any bright future for the misfits of this world. So it is with human beings, whether poor or affluent. They seek in this world a satisfaction which escapes them no matter how avidly they seek it.

It may be that those who are longing for contentment do not know the difference between the peace of this world and the peace of God. Jesus pointed out that two types of peace exist when he said to his disciples, "My peace I give to you; not as the world gives do I give to you." What did he mean by this?

There is a peace that the world gives. It is a light and frothy happiness typically sought by every good-time Charlie who seeks money and enjoys drink and sex. It may be found more respectably among those who exalt the arts and seek meaning from them. Sometimes those who preach the peace of this world adopt the ways of religion. Some people turn to Transcendental Meditation and other pychological self-help approaches. Such quiet meditation and mind control are supposed to do wonders for the human spirit, but one doubts their lasting effect.

There is some satisfaction in the peace which the world gives, however. Everyone enjoys a good dinner, a new suit or dress, a good night's rest, an evening with friends, money for pleasure, sporting events, etc. But unfortunately these things have never been endowed by the Creator with power to grant us lasting satisfaction. At best they provide only a passing peace which is gone in a moment. It will not stand the test of time.

Earlier in my years I knew a young man who was quite rich. He was a grandson of one of America's wealthiest families, but his mother was in a mental institution and his father was living with a fourth or fifth wife. The young man was attractive and very likeable. He was inheriting money from his grandfather's estate in huge chunks annually and had traveled extensively all over the world as a result of this privileged position. Here at home his life was spent in a series of attempts to find joy. One month he would shoot pheasant in South Dakota. The next month he might be skiing. But all of it was to no avail. He was an unhappy man. In addition, illnesses seemed to besiege his family. There was a constant attempt to find some climate where they could live in health. So, in rich gypsy fashion, he and his family traipsed across the world. He was a likeable and friendly person yet so miserable! As I talked with him and listened to him, I sensed again the truth that the peace which this world gives is not enough.

In contrast to the peace of the world, the peace of God has genuine satisfaction in it. When you find God you drink cool water that quenches your thirst. Or, to change the metaphor, you are at home with and enjoy communion with God, a relationship no earthly power can take away from you.

Eugene O'Neill wrote a play which has the title

"Days Without End." It is the one play in which O'Neill considers the cross. A man whose name is John Loving, after bitter personal failure, finds himself early one morning beneath the crucifix in the chapel of a small church. The good part of him is struggling with the evil part. The author, using a Greek literary device, separates the one man into two, and the two figures struggle beneath the cross. At the end, the good man triumphs over the evil one. When one reads this play, one might have cause to think of how tragic it was that O'Neill never discovered in his own life what the cross offers. Had he done so, he might have been spared the torment of his later years.

A relationship to God is the all-important thing, and we must understand what it involves. Paul Tournier has helped us at this point. In his book, *The Healing of Persons,* he makes this statement, "Behind all personal problems there lies sin."[1] It may startle you to read such words from a physician, but Paul Tournier believes that confession of sin is the front door which leads to inner peace.

This truth can be documented with countless examples. If the problem is that of marital difficulty, in all probability there lies beneath it some sin. If the problem is one of personal relationships, the chances are that there is some sin which has gone unrecognized and unconfessed. It is the confession of sin followed by the forgiveness of God and a new life which leads to the peace of God within.

I am aware that this spiritual fact can be overstated, and I must be careful not to do so. I'm not even sure I agree with Dr. Tournier completely since some misfortunes such as incurable disease cannot be attributed to sin. Yet, much of our heartache is rooted in our personal failures before God. When sin is confessed with true penitence and forgiven, the result is sweet release from burdens we have already borne too long!

The restless state is known, however, not only by the unbeliever but also by the one who calls himself Christian. Why is it that many who know of Christ remain dissatisfied? Here we recognize that there is such a thing as Christian discontent. This reveals itself in the lives of men like John Wesley who on May 24, 1738, on a Wednesday evening at about a quarter of nine, felt his heart strangely warmed with the presence of God. He felt his sins forgiven and his heart filled with love. Yet on May 26, only two days later, we find him writing in his journal, "My soul continued in peace, yet in heaviness because of manifold temptations." He wrote that the tempter had caused him to doubt his experience, suggesting, "this cannot be faith; or where is thy joy?"[2]

What we have here is the dissatisfaction of non-Christian and Christian alike—but with a difference. In one instance, there is no awareness of any relationship with God. In the other, there is. Christians know that they are loved whether they feel satisfied always or not. They are like fretful children who know parental love though that love may seem to be hard on them at times, causing them to be restless. And, they know, too, that religious feeling comes in alternating currents. You cannot always *feel* forgiven and loved, but you can live in this truth and know many high moments of fellowship with God.

Look also at the fact that there is a difference in the peace of the world and the peace of God as it affects the Christian. The Hebrew word for peace in the Bible is "shalom." It never means the absence of trouble. It means whatever makes for our highest good. In contrast, the peace which the world offers is the peace of escape, the peace which comes from avoidance of trouble and often from a refusal to face life's demands. The peace which Jesus offers us is the peace of conquest. Though we meet things head on, it is a peace which no experience in life can ever take from us.

Broadly speaking, we might say that there is a dissatisfaction for the earthbound and the heaven-bound. The latter is far more glorious and rewarding than the former. Take the prodigal son as an example. While he was at home in his father's house he was restless. But when he wasted his substance and found himself in want far from home, he was restless all the more. Later he returned to his father's house in true contrition. There, acceptance and peace came to him. There would still be moments when he would chafe under the restraining life of a son, but he had discovered that dissatisfaction in his father's house was far more rewarding than dissatisfaction amid the pleasures of sin.

So the Christian's feeling of unworthiness about himself can be a door to inner peace if he looks at himself humbly, is always mindful of his sins, and seeks to overcome them. Strangely enough, it is in this state that the peace of God comes, not in some state of self-righteous spiritual attainment. Paul, who knew wonderfully the peace of God, wrote "Christ Jesus came into the world to save sinners. And I am the foremost of sinners" (I Tim. 1:15).

In our quest for peace, dissatisfaction with ourselves is our greatest ally in sensing God's presence. John Hutton, a British minister, reminds us of this in a sermon he entitled "The Blessedness of Moral Sorrow." Whenever God seemed nowhere around, Hutton was able to find him or be found by him when he took a survey of his life and humbly realized his moral failures. Then God became a living presence again, granting him, as a result of his humility and trust, the blessedness of his peace.

The doors of peace are open to us. Confession of our sins brings God near, and an abiding sense of unworthiness produces a humility that sends us after God anew. Along this road of struggle and discovery is the contentment we seek.

5

Your Security Blanket

*Faith is standing in the darkness and a hand is there, and
we take it.*

—Keith Miller, *The Becomers*

All of us know the importance of the word
"security." We refer to the stocks and bonds that we
possess as securities. Our houses are protected by
security systems, made safe by security locks, and
kept under surveillance by security patrols. In high
government circles we refer to national security.
And, there is Social Security.

This protective need is expressed for us in
popular form in one of the characters created by
Charles Schulz in his comic strip, *Peanuts*. Linus
possesses a security blanket which is very dear to
him. In one of the episodes, Snoopy snatches the
security blanket from Linus and flies through the
door in cold midwinter with Linus suspended in
midair holding onto the blanket for dear life.
Outside in the snow, a battle ensues. At last Linus
wins, clutches his blanket, and stands exhausted at
the front door. His sister, Lucy, admonishes him,
"Are you crazy? It is cold outside! You could catch
pneumonia rolling around out there in the snow."
Linus replies, "The struggle for security knows no
season!"[1] And it doesn't! Much of our daily effort is
directed toward making and keeping ourselves
secure, providing security blankets for ourselves.

In one sense this is good. In fact, it is a necessity. We do need to feel secure in this life. But in another sense, it is harmful—particularly if as adults we remain like Linus. The friends of Linus seek to remove his security blanket because it indicates an unwillingness on his part to face up to the demands of life. They want Linus to grow up and be able to manage his life successfully. Thus they see the security blanket as having to go.

Most parents have known this experience with their children, and they know how difficult it is to remove an object on which a child depends. I knew a couple who had one son who did not want to move beyond the thumb-sucking, ear-twiddling, blanket-clutching age, all of which he did simultaneously. The child could not sleep and would hardly eat without his blanket. The parents decided to rid him of the blanket by cutting off a small piece at a time. They kept this up until finally the blanket was reduced to a small patch, and the dependency was ended. This couple was wise to help the child by this procedure. There is great trauma in suddenly being deprived of things on which one has depended. If they can be removed a step at a time, the trauma may be reduced.

In confronting this problem, we should recognize that at times we are all very stubborn about growing up. In fact, some people never reach maturity and remain emotional cripples all of their lives. None of us ever grows up completely. There is always a bit of the child in the adult, and this is wholesome. It adds spice to our living. But, we must be mature enough to manage our affairs if we are to live successfully.

One of the defense mechanisms we use to hold on to our blankets of security is to rationalize our weaknesses. We defend them by inventing good excuses, like Linus who says, "Only one yard of outing flannel stands between me and a nervous breakdown."[2] That was not true, of course, but Linus was convinced that this was the case.

On another occasion Charlie Brown asks him, "What if everyone was like you? What if we all ran away from our problems? Huh? What then? What if everyone in the whole world suddenly decided to run away from his problems?" Linus clutches his blanket more closely, sucks his thumb, then replies, "Well, we would all be running in the same direction."[3] How easy it is to defend our weaknesses when we are threatened with losing them. It is more comfortable to remain as we are than to make the effort necessary to explore the unfamiliar.

Such weakness and dependency provide hideouts for us; life becomes arrested at the dependency level. Sometimes parents encourage their children to remain dependent, particularly if a parent-child relationship is initiated to answer a parent's need. That is always dangerous. There is a maternal and paternal instinct which makes us want to have children. But if a mother or father is so insecure that the child is needed for their own security, the child is the security blanket, and the parent won't let go! This presents an intolerable situation which can be very destructive to a child's growth patterns.

Early in my ministry a young girl asked me if I would perform her marriage to a young man with whom she had fallen in love. She was a senior in college but was the victim of a possessive mother who had been making all of her decisions, even buying her clothes. The mother had chosen her college and her vocation. The daughter was to go into medicine, and the mother had lined up a place for her in the office of a family friend. So when this lovely young lady had fallen in love with a student who was studying for the ministry, her mother had rejected her daughter's choice. The girl was most distraught when she came to see me. I agreed to conduct the ceremony if I could see her and her fiancé on two or three occasions for premarital counseling. They came faithfully, and at the conclusion of the sessions the wedding was performed in the chapel of the church. She bought her own trousseau on the advice of her college counselor. The staff of the church were witnesses and also provided the wedding cake! We wanted to do everything in proper order since we knew the telephone lines would soon burn with the anger of a rejected mother. But as this lovely young woman said to me, "My very future as a person is at stake in this decision." When the mother received the word, she called and gave my secretary a good tongue-lashing as expected. But after a few minutes she settled down and began to ask sensible questions. She wanted to know the color of her daughter's dress, where she purchased it, etc. My secretary very wisely told her of all the events leading up to the wedding. I do not think that the mother has ever accepted the young couple, but I have seen them across the years, and they are quite happy. In this case, the need of a parent to lean heavily on a child almost destroyed the child. The security blanket had to be removed, and the daughter did it. Whether the mother learned anything from this experience I never found out.

The way we meet our need for security can be crucial for the success of married life. Though they are adults, some husbands and wives act like babies. They make the same demands on each other that infants do of parents. They expect their total needs to be met by the other. They drain each other for all they can get. One young woman discussed such a condition with her counselor. She was married to a very immature and pampered young man. When the session was about over, the counselor asked her what she planned to do. She replied, "I am going to bundle up this overgrown baby and send him back to his mother!" The refusal of a person to grow into adulthood, with the accompanying demands this places on others, produces situations which are intolerable for many people. We must become mature people if we are to handle those experiences which demand maturity. We should not accept any security that provides a cop-out for us emotionally.

The kind of security blanket we provide for ourselves is most important. What kind of security can we expect the Christian faith to offer us? You can be sure that the security blanket which God provides does not coddle us. God wants us to be whole, mature people who are finding his purpose in the lives we live with love for ourselves and others. In other words, he wishes us to become, in time, mature adults.

But while God will not coddle us, he does provide us with a security blanket. Listen to this reassuring line from Psalm 16: "Preserve me, O God, for in thee I take refuge" (v. 1). This prayer might sound like a weak man praying for God to surround him in his weakness, but this was David who fought Goliath with a slingshot and slew him, the David who was now king of Israel, a leader of her armies in battle. In other words, it is not a weak man wanting to be reassured as he continues to be weak. Rather, it is a man who, though strong, does have weaknesses. In this case, it is the temptations of the flesh. David also knows his needs as he experiences the loneliness of leadership, so he asks God for help to make him strong.

Or take another example, that of Paul the great apostle. In his Letter to the Ephesians he prays "that according to the riches of his glory he may grant you to be strengthened with might through his Spirit in the inner man" (3:16). Here is a noble saint who saw the possibilities of Christ in the human heart rooting and grounding us in love and giving us a comprehension of all of the dimensions of life. He was not a weak man who wanted to remain weak. He had some sort of disability in the flesh; he knew what it was to fear for his life; he knew defeat in moral struggle, and it was in the midst of this battle that he wanted God's strength.

And there is another great Christian, the apostle Peter. Here are his words to those entrusted in his care: "Cast all your anxieties on him, for he cares about you" (I Peter 5:7). Again we have the picture of a great leader who knows anxious moments but also is aware of the overpowering presence of God. This is the man who could stand before a crowd of hostile people to preach a moving sermon that won many converts. Here is a man who in prison could say to a powerful ruler who urged him to recant, "We must obey God and not men."

Jesus himself demonstrates this combination of strength and dependence: "Now is my soul troubled. And what shall I say? 'Father, save me from this hour'? No, for this purpose I have come to this hour" (John 12:27). Again it is the picture of one who will not turn from his appointed task though he is troubled in spirit. As the Father's Son, he knows the comfort of the Father's presence. Likewise, even the strongest of us will need God to sustain us. Is this weakness? Some think so and do not like to surrender themselves to anyone. They want to be self-contained units of resourcefulness. But keep in mind that God's desire to help us is not that we should remain weak but that he might make us strong. He will help you to your feet and enable you to stand, but it is you who must stand by his help. This is the right kind of dependence, for it leads not to further regression but to greater strength.

You cannot avoid being dependent on God. Your very being and daily existence depend on him. You need only feel your pulse to note the life force flowing through you that is not of your own making. If you accept this dependence of your body, why should you be concerned that you display weakness in calling on God with your problems of spirit? In either instance his creative power is available for you.

Vincent Collins revised the first edition of his book *Me, Myself, and You* to include a chapter on "Me, Myself, and God" in the second edition. He had been reluctant to write of God in the first edition. In the foreword to the second, he says that earlier he did not want to seem like "holy Joe" or use God as a therapeutic agent. He thought that this might turn people off. But after hearing from many people, he changed his mind and chose to express his faith. In the foreword to the revised edition he writes, "You will find a new section in this book entitled 'Me and God.' I make no apologies for it—after all, emotional maturity is complete acceptance of reality. He is the supreme reality."[4] And so he is! If we understand him correctly and pray to him as the source of our being, if we depend on the presence of his spirit like we depend on the sunshine and the rain, we shall know what makes for our maturity. Having found *the* security blanket with the proper dimensions, we can then throw the old one away.

6

Keep on Walking

The best way out is always through.
—Robert Frost, *A Servant to Servants*

For all of us there is a desired quality of life called true grit. It is the capacity to walk life's road with an abiding courage. A man I know who is in serious financial trouble said to me recently, "I have to get up each day and keep going. There is nothing else I can do." That was a display of true grit. He could throw in the towel and call it quits, but he chooses to do otherwise and is to be commended for it.

There are many people who walk in courage every day. Every fall thousands of college freshmen must make their own way in a new venture. Some people battle fear, insecurity, and loneliness on college campuses. Others, more self-assured, find themselves having to deal with a new freedom which is theirs. Both must face their experiences and see them through in terms of their own personal growth. Or consider those who have long been on the road—our older citizens. Their muscles are not as strong; their minds are not as alert. They know that much of their road is behind them, yet they must keep walking.

There is also the person who is emotionally troubled. Afraid, uncertain, depressed, he must still go on. One of the noblest of all human qualities is that of keeping on, even when the going is tough. I don't know where you find yourself in this saga of human experience, but I'm sure you understand what I mean.

Each of us needs an inner toughness. This is one of life's demands. Often it is given to us by our parents, and if this has been your lot you are fortunate indeed. Strong, stable parents have a good chance of producing stable children. It is a blessed thing to grow up in a family where one hears parents say, "Don't whine and complain! Never say can't! Face what you fear! Be considerate of others! Have good manners. Practice politeness." How rewarding it is to learn such attitudes from one's parents.

Unfortunately, many of us have to find this stability and toughness on our own. It isn't easy, but it can be done. I know an emotionally insecure young lady who married but did not assume responsibility in her role. She was far too dependent on her mother and father. She didn't make it as a partner in marriage, and the divorce which resulted only added to her emotional struggles. Another lady cut the umbilical cord, even though she found it difficult. While she still loves her family very much, she is building a new life with her husband and children.

Consider the neurotic person whose own behavior baffles him. Some of it just doesn't make sense—why is he overly anxious, bordering on a state of panic, and sometimes acting erratically? Some do nothing about this state, as miserable as they are. They cling to others, start every conversation with a personal problem of their own, and make no bold advances to manage their affairs. But others are different. They develop a toughness toward themselves. They will not coddle their neuroses. They do what they ought whether the feeling is there or not.

When I think of inner toughness, I remember reading about a noted warrior who lived many centuries ago when men fought their battles with swords and shields. On the eve of a conflict, this great man looked at his hands and saw that they trembled. His stout spirit reacted: "Tremble on; you would tremble more if you knew where I will take you today!" Such is the toughness needed for the road ahead.

We must also be ready for changes in scenery along the way. We move through one scene after another, in job, health, and the aging process. Some steps we cannot help; others we can do something about. However, many find it extremely difficult to make adjustments, and they develop all sorts of neurotic fears.

Look for a moment at the fact that both men and women go through a "change of life." This is a well-known turning point, and some of it is physical. Much of it, however, is a psychological reaction to the physical. A man who approaches forty, or is just beyond, goes through changes. His hair gets thin; he becomes paunchy around the middle; he notices that he doesn't bounce back as rapidly after a hard day's work. He slows down sexually. He begins to notice the obituary column in the newspaper. He realizes that he is in the high-risk heart attack group.

So he worries and worries, and unconsciously his behavior patterns and interests begin to change. He develops irrational fears, and these drive him to do things which he would not do otherwise. He may overdo it in acting young. To prove his sexual virility, he might have an affair. He grows jealous of those with whom he works, especially the young. This man is going through climacteric change.

The process is similar in women. They reach an age when they can no longer bear children, and they see in this a loss of youthfulness. To be on the eve of menopause puts many women in a state of shock. Some panic. They worry too much about their looks and are mystified by their feelings of irritability and insecurity which are often accompanied by the well-known hot flashes.

At this point many seek help in counseling, a wise decision after medical problems have been checked. Some discover what is happening to them by reading good books in the field of growth and personality change. In any event, the important thing is to make peace with this stage and live through it. Nothing is to be gained by resisting it.

We should keep all of this in mind when we are dealing with the irrational ills of our friends and loved ones. In one of his books, Bruce Larson writes of a conversation with a psychiatrist. The psychiatrist said, "I am convinced that there is no such thing as mental illness. What we call mental illness is only an attempt to grow. In trying to restore the patient to a former state, the doctor and the family often do more harm than good. If we can identify and live with him through this time of growth, he will emerge a better person, more mature, and more whole."[1]

This really is our aim, isn't it? It will help some dear one very little if in trying to cure his mental problems we arrest his development at the point of his trouble. Instead, just as in the change of life, we should do all we can to help him grow through this experience and emerge on the other side a much stronger person prepared for the present and future which lie before him.

As we walk through this life our goals should be reexamined and altered when necessary. What a person's goals are at the age of twenty might be vastly different from what they are at forty, fifty, or seventy. Some things that are accomplished early in life give way to an interest in others. Perhaps a good maxim might be, "Never fear to give away a dream of youth which has been realized in order that you may dream again." Such an attitude certainly keeps us alive to the present moment and gives us an exciting pilgrimage.

This point is well made by Henry David Thoreau in his writings from Walden Pond. Thoreau left Concord, Massachusetts, and went to the woods to live a certain life-style. With his own hands he built a cabin, and in the midst of nature he thought and wrote while supporting himself through his own toil. After two years in the woods, he returned to city life. He describes this decision in these words: "I left the woods for as good a reason as I went there. Perhaps it seemed to me that I had several more lives to live, and could not spare any more time for that one."[2] This is a good example of how each of us finishes certain steps in his life and goes on to take others. It is very important that we recognize this inevitability. If you find yourself all uptight emotionally, you might ask yourself if you are resisting some inevitable change in your life. If so, you must let go in order to live life's next episode as happily as you ought.

We should sense that this provides life with its real excitement. If we can continue to look toward tomorrow, this will keep us open to new moments and events. This was true of Pablo Casals, the world-renowned cellist. At age ninety-three on his birthday he said, "Every day I am reborn, every day is a new lifetime for me." What a marvelous point of view for a man who had about come to the end of his pilgrimage. He had lived beyond his appointed time. Thus, every day was a new life for him. He received it as such and used it gloriously.

Such an attitude saves us from enslavement to memories. Attachment to the past becomes neurotic for many people. They simply cannot let go. This is described for us in Charles Schulz's comic strip characters. Snoopy the dog has great fondness for the past, particularly for the Daisy Hill Puppy Farm. Periodically he makes a visit to his first home. On one occasion Snoopy returns only to discover that the Puppy Farm has been replaced by a parking garage. As the cars go in and out Snoopy cries, "I can't stand it! You stupid people! You are parking on my memories!"

Isn't part of our problem that we resent other people parking on our memories? This is one of the causes for the present generation gap. Those of us a little older look back to the good old days or the very bad old days and say to the young of this generation, "You don't really know how it was!" With nostalgia, we return to those years when life was simple and bemoan the fact that this is not true today. Or, in the midst of an economic recession, we think of how terrible the great depression was in the late twenties and early thirties. When someone pays us no attention, we sense that they are being insensitive about our memories. Memories are precious, but they must not enslave us. However wonderful they were during one part of our journey, they are now gone and we must keep on walking. Life lies ahead, not in a past that is gone.

This means that the past must be healed. It must release us to the present and to the future, or we become enslaved. If this is your problem, look honestly at your past. Confront it for what it was. Then having benefited from what you have learned, just as quickly let it go. Leave it in God's hands. This does not mean that you will forever forget it or never return to it in your thoughts. Quite the contrary. You may return to it on occasion, but you will see it as a phase of your life beyond which you have now moved. If the past has been sacred and beautiful, you will remember it as such, but you will sense that life can no longer be lived there. If the past has been hostile, you must leave this, too. You will be living for the present with new goals set for the future.

Let me now come to the most important thing of all about this changing pilgrimage. As you walk through this life, remember that you do not walk alone. There are others who walk with you, and above all there is the presence of God.

When Abraham Lincoln was leaving Springfield, Illinois, for Washington to begin another chapter in his life, some friends gathered to see him off. Among them was a dear Quaker woman who called him "Friend Abraham" and whispered into his ear that God would surely go with him. This was a great comfort to the new president. As we undertake each step of our journey we should know, too, that there is one who is our "friend," the Holy Spirit, who whispers in our hearts the message of his love. He will surely go with us to give us the help we need.

As Elton Trueblood puts it, God is not one who is discussed and argued about but one who is encountered. Trueblood uses the Twenty-third Psalm to point this out. First in this psalm God is spoken about: "He maketh me to lie down in green pastures." But in the fourth verse the mood changes: "Yea, though I walk through the valley of the shadow of death, I will fear no evil; *for Thou art with me*." There is a radical change here for now the matter has become quite personal. Trueblood goes on to say, "What it means is that at the profoundest depths men talk not about God but with Him."[3] How true!

Again and again this truth appears in those

people who have found the courage to believe. I met a woman a few years ago when her doctor asked me to visit her in the hospital. He told me that she had no physical illness which could not be cured, but that she had lost her will to live. Troubles had piled upon her to such a degree that she no longer had the strength to deal with them. Though she was in her mid-forties, she felt that no one cared for her and that her life was over. On my first visit I simply got acquainted with her and tried to show her that I was interested in her as a person. She was a very frail individual. Unable to retain food, she had to be fed intravenously. She weighed less than a hundred pounds, and it seemed certain that unless her attitude about herself and life changed she would surely die.

As one visit followed another, I began to see a little light in her eyes. We talked of her life, her hurts, her needs. We talked about human experience, how tough it is, but how great a challenge it is. We talked of the fact that all individuals experience difficulty of one sort or another. Then we talked about faith in God and about his eternal care. We prayed together. Slowly but surely she began to make her way back. She reached a point where she could eat soft foods, and soon she was gaining weight and sensed that her strength was returning. Above all, her attitude toward life changed dramatically.

I remember the Easter Sunday morning when I arose early for church services. It had been a dark and rainy night, and it was still pouring rain at the early morning hour. Outside there were no rays of light, and I wondered whether we would have many people at the services. When I finished my breakfast and had dressed for the day, I was making final preparations to leave when the phone rang. It was her voice from the hospital room. She was calling to wish us a good day at the church. Then she added, "Though it's dark and rainy outside, I just want to tell you that my sun is still up!" I knew then that she was going to be all right. She had bordered on despair, but with God's help, she discovered that she could make it. Such are the benefits of faith. However difficult the way might be, with his help, we know that we can make it through.

7

Dealing with Grief

We intend to die by this faith; why should we not live by it?
—Martin Luther

"For everything there is a season, and a time for every matter under heaven: . . . a time to weep, and a time to laugh; a time to mourn, and a time to dance" so wrote Ecclesiastes, the Preacher (3:1, 4). If laughing and dancing are a part of our earthly lot, so are weeping and mourning.

This sentiment is also echoed in the New Testament in many places, but in one spot in particular, the sixth chapter of Luke, in his account of the Sermon on the Mount. Jesus, having spent a night in prayer in the hills, comes down to greet his disciples. He begins to preach and among other things says, "Woe to you that are full now, for you shall hunger. Woe to you that laugh now, for you shall mourn and weep" (v. 25).

Such words introduce us to that universal condition we call grief. By this I do not mean that superficial thing that goes in the name of grief. A child who cries over a broken toy, an athlete who weeps over a lost sporting event, or a housewife who weeps because she has had a fretful day—we can understand; but such tears do not point to deep, poignant grief. A classic biblical example along the same lines is Ahab turning his face to the wall, sulking, and refusing to eat because he could not gain access to Naboth's vineyard. He grieved selfishly for what was owned by another man, but the matter was not crucial to his welfare. It only made him pout.

There is, however, an existential grief. It reaches deep until like the psalmist we cry, "My days are like an evening shadow; I wither away like grass" (102:11). Such heartache may be caused by the loss of a loved one—husband, wife, parent, or child. This is the most common form of grief and some are completely overcome by it. How does one handle it? How should a Christian approach existential grief?

Before seeking a true Christian answer, let us look at some of the unwholesome ways in which people deal with grief. One way is that of complete defeat, utter dejection, a giving up. Sometimes these abject feelings spring from guilt. A person may have failed to be good to another. He may indeed have wronged that person and may have driven him to an early grave. When death occurs, there is then an agony of conscience sometimes accompanied by flagellation of self. This is an effort to do penance by grieving and spurning happiness. Any psychiatrist knows that funeral tears may often be those of remorse rather than love.

Closely allied to this is the case of one who loves but is remorseful over failure to express that love. Now the opportunity is gone. "If I had just taken the time to say, 'I love you,'" he laments. Erich Segal wrote a book called *Love Story*. It was made into a movie, and many cried their way through it. It is a sad story of two young lovers, Oliver and Jenny, who have an illicit love affair that turns into marriage. Late in the story she dies of leukemia. Oliver's father, not really understanding his son, appears at the last in the hospital to offer help—financial and otherwise. "Jenny's dead," Oliver says plainly. "I'm sorry," his father whispers, stunned. Then Oliver quotes Jenny, "Love means not ever having to say you're sorry."[1]

There is a degree of truth here, of course, but this does not and cannot mean that we love each other perfectly or that we are held accountable in conscience for such. Sometimes grief at this point comes from remorse at having left the hospital room, even if for a needed lunch, during which time a loved one dies. We were not there, and it hurts. Thank God some are fortunate enough to have those last moments. Others fail and later grieve. In all of these cases good sense must prevail. Had we known the time and the hour, we most certainly would have been there. But how is one to know? And where wrong was actually done to another, it does no good to grieve endlessly over one's guilt. Confess the guilt. Receive God's forgiveness, and then let the past lie at rest.

When this dejection springs from genuine love it still does us no good to pine our lives away in unrelieved gloom, resisting every effort of friends and loved ones to persuade us to do otherwise. True, grief needs to be expressed, but not unendingly. Sometimes one feels that by grieving one is being faithful to the loved one now gone. Although this is better than the casual air that

71

suggests one never really loved, ultimately it is a self-sacrificing love that becomes distorted. Is this really what a departed loved one wants of us? Constant, agonizing grief? It would seem that such pain would only add to theirs. There is the temptation to throw in the towel and say, "My life is finished. We had planned it all together; now he is gone. I don't see how I can go on and really don't want to go on without him." Those are the terrible consequences of separation. But then one senses that life must continue. There are others to be considered—brothers, sisters, children, dear friends. They care. They love us. Unrelieved gloom is not faithful to the dead or to the living. We must resist such feelings and know that God bids us to live. Reasons for doing so become plain as we allow time and prayer to heal.

Another unproductive response to the loss of a loved one is to let grief turn to anger. There exists in a church I know a very fine and active organization called WHO—We Help Others; We Help Ourselves. This group consists mainly of those who have lost loved ones by death. When they were first organized, their counselor, a wise man, suggested the possibility that some might be angry with God because of the loss of their dear ones. Immediately there were denials, and perhaps those who protested were right. But anger toward God is a subtle thing. It often masquerades under some other form, as do many of our moods. A father may come home at night, weary and frustrated, and take out his tensions on one of his children who bothers him.

Actually he is not angry at the child but at himself or someone who has irked him during the day.

In the same manner, anger toward God, though not obvious, may be present. Let a loved one die and anger may be directed at medicine bottles, doctors, or nurses. That is always an unprofitable approach and is even more upsetting when we realize that it is God with whom we are put out.

But what a pity to throw God away in anger and add this loss to one already bitter and hard! Loss of loved ones, however difficult, must be accepted. Rebellion hardens the heart. We must forgive the loss. It may take time and prayer, but it must be done.

In addition, we must come to a sound belief and trust in God. One of the fondest memories of my boyhood days is that of missionaries and their families who came to visit our church. One such family was the Towsons. Their son, Hatton, was an honor graduate of Emory University and a Rhodes Scholar at Oxford. After he had completed his studies abroad, he was assigned to a small church in south Georgia. But his ministry was to come to an end almost before it began. Hatton died in a small-town hospital during surgery for an inflamed appendix. When it happened, Mrs. Towson, a saint of God, said to my mother with an unfaltering trust, "My Father did it and it's all right."

That's a beautiful trust, but did God really do it? Did he will it? Again we are at the door of the awful mystery of evil. And again I, for one, must say that I do not believe that God wills such catastrophe, though in some mysterious way it exists in his universe. Actually, death may be caused by self-neglect or the mistakes of others. Let us not lay it forever at God's door. Rather, let us say, "Our Father didn't do it or will it, though it is somehow allowed; but because he loves us and cares for us, it is all right." That's much better theology.

Let us also have faith to believe that out of this most awful pain some good may come. J. Carter Swaim, in his book *Body, Soul, and Spirit,* tells of Elton Trueblood giving lectures only a few days after his first wife's death.[2] The great Christian had insisted on keeping the date. As he spoke, he said that if he had to give up all the Bible except one text, he would hold onto the words, "We know that in everything God works for good with those who love him, who are called according to his purpose" (Rom. 8:28). I can certainly understand this. The words give us needed comfort. The phrase "in everything" is a very important one, for it means "in all times and places." That includes the now and the future. God supplies our needs today and tomorrow. Of this we can be sure. If you doubt it, just put God to the test. Throw yourself on his mercy and love and see if he will not come to your aid. Millions testify that he does and will.

C. S. Lewis helps us with this matter of trust. In his book *Letters to an American Lady,* published posthumously, he wrote that he was asked by his American correspondent how he handled sorrow after a personal tragedy. His wife, the noted Joy Davidson, had died two months earlier of cancer.

His answer was, "As to how I take sorrow, the answer is, 'in nearly all the possible ways.' Because, as you probably know, it isn't a state but a process. It keeps on changing—like a winding road with quite a new landscape at each hand."[3] So it is. The effects of our grief change. It will be one thing now, another later. It helps to expect this and to know that at every change of the landscape God is present.

So we ask again, What good may come out of sorrow? A new seriousness, for one thing, a profound belief that while death is real so is heaven. We may also develop a new tenderness toward others. We may sense that we will be saved by losing ourselves in their needs. We realize also a new life demand for personal strength and character. And when death is accepted, we feel a closer relationship with God. We are given a new life with him with new possibilities. Don't ever forget: when one door closes in life, God always opens another. He will do that for you if you trust him.

Such attainments will not come all at once. They will come as the road opens ahead. Don't look too far into the future. As John Henry Newman put it in his hymn, "I do not ask to see the distant scene; one step enough for me."[4] This was a step preceded by a prayer, "Lead kindly Light, amid th' encircling gloom." This is precisely the spot in which you may find yourself. It may be dark all around, but in that darkness there is the kindly light of God's loving presence. He will help you take the next step. Then grief, while still with you, will have lost its terrible sting. You will be left with memories of lovely days with your dear one for which you will remain forever thankful. Beyond all this, you will have found the courage to live again.

8

Don't Lose Heart

If one lives for a long time immersed in God's grace there stretches across one's soul a calm which nothing can destroy.
—Toyohiko Kagawa

There are certain experiences in this life that are common to us all. Among other things, we hunger, thirst, desire to be loved, want creative work and time for fun and relaxation. And—we all have troubles. All of us will feel dejected at times and will be tempted to lose heart.

When we ask why this is so, there seem to be many reasons. One cause is an overabundance of work and the frustrations related thereto. Most everyone has seen on someone's desk or office wall these words: "The harder I work the behinder I get!" Some people are too heavily loaded with work, and they never catch up. They are like the farmer who was asked what time he went to work. He replied that he didn't go to work; he awoke in the middle of it! One can get depressed under such conditions. Then there is the task of making ends meet on what we earn. Two fellows were talking and one asked the other, "How do you spend your income?" The other replied, "Thirty percent for housing, 30 percent for clothing, 40 percent for food, and 20 percent for recreation." The first man reacted, "That can't be! That's 120 percent!" The second responded, "Don't I know it!" Many of us know this plight, for sure.

A loss of heart over such matters may be a mild dejection which soon passes with a good night's rest, a few days off, a raise in pay, a good meal, or a better golf game. But at times this troubled feeling can be so acute and so stubbornly unyielding that it results in a loss of meaning and a sense of defeat in one's life. People who feel this way are like the man who was at a bookshop in an airport. He saw a large number of self-help books on the stands. When he commented on this, the saleswoman, a precocious person, said, "Yes, we carry a lot of these books. The people who buy them are puzzled, defeated, afraid, and tired of fighting. They seek between the covers of a book some word of hope." There is a lot of truth in that statement. Notice the faces of people you meet on the streets, in air terminals, or even at sporting events. Notice how drained some of them seem to be.

In this matter no age is spared. Those who have grown old lose heart when they face illnesses or the specter of what lies ahead. The middle-aged person becomes frustrated over the passing years or the towering responsibility of rearing and educating children. Matrimony feels the pressure also. Some marriages become endurance contests. Romance has faded and former lovers are tempted to lose heart. The young certainly have their frustrations surrounding their life's work, marriage, and something they can believe in and depend upon. A noted writer once said, "Thank God, we can never suffer again as we did in our youth." Whether we are young or old, the struggle goes on.

What can be done about such conditions so that we do not lose heart? For one thing, there must be a degree of realism about our living that helps us to accept who we are and what we are capable of doing. Some people expect everything to be right in this world, but it isn't and it won't be! Some people do not expect enough of themselves, but others expect the impossible and this brings distress. Expect a lot but not that impossible "everything." Today the child's question is, "What's happened to my world?" The young adult says, "Stop the world, I want to get off!" The older person laments, "Things are moving too fast for me!" Yet we can't get off the world or slow things down unless we leave life behind, and there's no hope in that. This means, surely, that we can't be responsible for the whole world, only our part of it.

The noted Christian physician Paul Tournier was once accused by a colleague of suffering from a distorted sense of responsibility. Tournier responded that he was not responsible for the whole world but, more modestly, for that small, immediate circle where he lived. Being faithful within those limits would produce the clear conscience. That is sound advice for living in this world. It is one way not to lose heart.

Also keep in mind that you can't play God. This was emphasized to a group of ministers once by a noted teacher of hospital chaplains. A chaplain himself, he revealed how he had come to handle his duties in that position. Before becoming a teacher, he had been employed in a large hospital. He described one week in particular when patient care had drained him unmercifully. He decided that he must have a break. As he walked out of the hospital, he turned, looked back, and thinking about his patients said, "I don't care if all of you die!" Why did he say this? He explained to the group still in shock that it was because he had taken upon himself the impossible burden of all of the patients, a responsibility which only God could assume. This was an abrupt choice of language to correct his error and put the responsibility where it belonged. He knew that he couldn't play God, so he learned to do his best and leave the rest with God.

When I went to my first pastorate, I drove there alone after seminary graduation. It was a bleak little parsonage to which I went as a single man. One light bulb hung from the ceiling in the living room, one in the bedroom, and one in the kitchen. Each functioned by a pull switch. There on the mantle I saw a letter from my predecessor who had gone into the army chaplaincy. In the letter he said to me, "This is a seven-point circuit. You will find more heartache here than perhaps you have at any other point in your life. Don't try to carry all of it alone. If you do, it will crush you. You will have to let God bear some of it." I hadn't been there a week before I knew what he was talking about. In my parish duties I discovered that there were many instances of disease and affliction. I remember some lovely young girls coming up with a horse-drawn cart selling vegetables. They were afflicted with a hereditary disease so deadly that when they reached their teens each of them slowly deteriorated and died. Yet that family was still producing children, each of whom was marked by the disease. Then there was an encephalitic infant whom I buried in a simple service. I can still see that child's father walking through the pine forest toward the cemetery carrying the small wooden box that contained the still body of his three-year-old. There was enough heartache in that pastorate to kill any man. Fortunately and of necessity, I realized that I could not be God. I had to put these matters into God's hands in order to survive. I was later to discover that my first pastorate was no different from others I would serve. The tragic parts of life are very real, and to survive one must put himself and those for whom he cares in God's hands.

This means that under all times and conditions we must know our limits. Edward Everett Hale puts it in these words:

> I am only one,
> But still I am one.
> I cannot do everything,
> But still I can do something;
> And because I cannot do everything,
> I will not refuse to do the something I can do.[1]

That's the only sensible way to live, doing the best you can and trusting God for the rest.

Acceptance of what we can be and do needs to be seen in the light of spiritual demands on us and in the light of God's grace. Here we might remember the apostle Paul who had attempted the impossible task of trying to please God with his life, only to fail. Then he found God's grace which showed him that he could never earn God's love but could only receive it freely through faith. From that time on, he began to live the Christian life out of gratitude.

We will always be frustrated and lose heart if we try to live a life completely perfect and pleasing to God. But, as Paul said, we do not lose heart if we see ourselves in another relationship with the Heavenly Father—the recipients of his Divine Grace which accepts us as we are. This gives us the courage to go on, doing our best.

During the days of neo-orthodox theology in seminary, students used a neo-orthodox phrase that could be easily misunderstood. They talked about "sinning bravely." That's dangerous language until you see that it means God loves us and receives us, and because he does, we can have the courage to live in spite of our imperfections. This doesn't mean life is less serious, but it gives us another direction—out from the center and not in toward the center of God's acceptance. Like Pogo in the comic strip, we are faced with insurmountable opportunities in the pursuit of which we will often fail, but we will not expect the impossible of ourselves any longer. We will have the courage to do our best because we are loved by God in spite of our imperfections. That takes the pressure off when accepted personally and lets us become our best selves out of gratitude for his love.

We need a positive faith. Even with an understanding of our situation and acceptance of it, we
are still open to disappointment and will need
healing. Understanding helps, but it is only part of
the solution. The danger is that many people stop
with the little peace that comes from honest
awareness of what bothers them. They must go
farther to take the steps of faith that are needed.

We lose heart at times because sin produces a
misspent life. If that sin is not remedied, we become
the victims of remorse or of a nagging and
burdening sense of guilt. This is demonstrated in
the life of Edgar Allen Poe who was a son of the
South and one of the nation's best-known poets. Poe
was a victim of his own thoughts and foolish sins. He
didn't know what to do with those sins. One night he
was found in an election booth, unconscious,
penniless, and a victim of alcohol. In his delirium
prior to death he cried out,

> O God . . . is all we see or seem
> but a dream within a dream?

Here was a genius who lacked the faith that would
have saved him had he acted on it.

A simple faith is needed to accept God's
forgiveness and be enabled to live again. Let's not
complicate it or distort it. It is strange how much
bizarre theology is being preached in movies today.
For instance, take the *Poseidon Adventure*. Like most
contemporary movies its language is raw, but it is
really a study of the atonement, the sacrificial death

of Jesus Christ. There is a priest in it who is very unorthodox. He teaches that there is a little bit of God in all of us that enables us to climb higher and higher. The *Poseidon* is a pleasure ship on cruise in the Mediterranean. An earthquake causes a sixty-foot tidal wave which turns the *Poseidon* upside down, killing or drowning most of the passengers. The story focuses on one group celebrating New Year's Eve in a ballroom. When the wave hits, the priest begs them to follow him to safety, but some won't go. (This is allegorical: some people don't follow Jesus Christ.) The priest pleads with them again and again and seems to know a way that others do not know. (Again the Jesus figure who said, "I am the way.") Some do follow the priest who is the Christ figure. He seems to know the exact turns to take (while others do not), and eventually they find their way to the ship's propeller where the hull is thinnest and they can cut their way through. But just at this moment steam begins to escape from around the large valve (painted red to symbolize the cross). The priest leaps to hang on the red wheel and seeks to turn it to stop the steam. It doesn't work. Then he pleads with God. "Don't kill them! Take me!" God accepts his sacrifice. The steam stops, but he, like Christ, cannot save himself and falls into the fire below. The people pound on the hull and are heard by those on the outside who cut through the metal and lead them to safety.

Obviously we have a theological point of view here: God is angry with the world and punishes it for its sins (the tidal wave). Someone has to appease his wrath. One man—Jesus—says, "Take me, and let these chosen (divine election) go free." God accepts the sacrifice, and they are released from sin and death. You may believe such theology, for many do, but it is cruel teaching. Is this really the nature of God? Does God send tidal waves to destroy human life because of our sinfulness? Does he demand a bloody sacrifice? There may be some truth in this view, but I prefer to believe that God *so loved the world—not hated it*—that he sent his only begotten Son that *whosoever*—not a few—believes in him should not perish but have everlasting life (John 3:16). That is the faith that keeps us from losing heart.

In one of his books, the late J. Wallace Hamilton tells of a big handsome athlete who went into his pastor's study with all his flags at halfmast. He told a sordid story of his sin against a lovely young girl and concluded the account in the language of the playing field: "I've been benched for foul play. Is there a chance for me, or must I sit out the rest of life's game on the sidelines?" The minister asked, "How old are you? That is, what quarter of the game is it?" "The first quarter," replied the boy. "And that means that there are still three quarters of the game to play?" "Yes, sir, three quarters." "And you really want to get back into the game?" "Yes, sir, if the coach will let me." "All right, son, let's get down on our knees and ask him."[2]

As Jesus said, "Your faith has made you whole; go in peace." Or, as Paul, in the light of God's grace, was moved to write, "So, we do not lose heart!" That way is open to all of us who have committed any wrong, and if we really accept God's love and forgiveness and forgive ourselves, we have exercised a faith that causes us not to lose hope.

9

Living with Tension

The best and most wonderful thing that can happen to you in this life, is that you should be silent and let God work and speak.

—Dag Hammarskjold, *Markings*

A well-known minister has observed that people are so uptight today that they can no longer sleep in church! This might well be, and it introduces a point. We are tension-ridden people who take aspirin for our headaches, tranquilizers for our nerves, and sleeping pills to make us sleep. We are told that more tranquilizers are sold than any other drug in the world.

This is not all bad, by any means. When properly taken, drugs can be a great help. The problem is that they deal with our stress on a surface level when what is needed is to get at the root causes and seek solution there. In any event, we must be concerned about tension since its toll upon our lives physically and emotionally, is becoming more and more obvious. It plays a prominent role in hypertension, heart attacks, gastro-intestinal disorders, and nervous problems. For this reason it cannot be ignored.

With all of this, however, there are those who feel that not much can be done about tension. It is the price we pay, they say, for living in this kind of a world. At best it can only be controlled. It cannot be removed.

There is a place for tension. It is a sign of life. Rigor mortis means that there is no longer any movement in our bodies. Death has come. So as long as there is life, there is some tension. The truth is that any job that excites us, tests us, and fulfills us is bound to produce some stress. The more responsibility we carry the more tense we might become. There are many who think that presidents of major corporations have it easy since they are able to call upon so many subordinates and have the privilege of planning their own time. What is not known is that such leaders carry with them every hour of the day the full load of responsibility for the organization they head. Let some major breakdown occur, and they, not workmen on the line, are held accountable. The most difficult position held in this nation is that of the presidency of the United States. What responsibility that office carries! I have seen pictures of our presidents when they have appeared to be physically exhausted. Most of them take frequent vacations, and we should understand that they could not bear such heavy burdens if they did not escape from them frequently. The job is pressure-ridden, yet very few men in that high office have not wanted to run for a second term. Obviously they find the task exhilarating.

This suggests something about tension as it appears within the lives of Christians. When one seeks to serve Christ one is sure to be extended in the endeavor, as was our Lord. Martin Luther, the great reformer, is a good example. He was faced with decisions which put him in opposition to the powers of the church. We are told that he suffered agonizing stomach distress. John Wesley, father of Methodism, faced the hostility of mobs which broke up his outdoor services. No doubt he felt threatened both in mind and body. Yet he could say to his ministers, "Always look a mob in the face!" In addition, Wesley faced marital stress since he was not compatible with the woman he married. There also lay upon him all the cares of the Methodist Societies. So it is certain that our greatest religious leaders knew stress. This means that when we treat tension within the Christian context, we do not mean the making of calm, placid, flattened out people who neither suffer nor know hardship. What we do mean is that real Christian heroes find the peace of God in the midst of struggle. If we are to be relieved from tension, peace will have to come to us in this fashion.

Let us see, too, that for Christians managing stress involves self-effort and the help of God. Some Christians have an aversion to introducing self-help into a situation which they feel could be resolved through faith in God. Some would toss aside the use of psychology, for example. They argue that our problems are resolved by trusting God alone. But such a picture is not true to the history of our faith. God does not do everything for us. We work with him to help ourselves. This is demonstrated in the life of the man who wrote and said the most about faith and trust, the apostle Paul. To a young man named Timothy, whom Paul considered to be his son in the faith, he wrote two letters which have been preserved for us in the Bible. In the second one he said to him, "You then, my son, be strong in the grace that is in Christ Jesus" (II Tim. 2:1). When Paul discovered that Timothy was timid and fearful in the presence of his elders, he urged him not to be ashamed of his youth. When he learned that Timothy suffered from stomach distress, he urged him to take a little wine for his problem. Thus Paul used both his good sense and his strong faith in giving help to Timothy. The fact is we are not disrespectful of God when we use the faculties which he has given us to help resolve our difficulties. These, together with our faith, can help us meet and overcome such problems as that of tension.

Let us now deal with the tenseness we so often feel in our lives. How are we to approach it? First, let me suggest that *we might avoid many of the situations which produce it.* The famed evangelist Dwight L. Moody was once approached by a man who was under the burden of a great problem. When he asked Moody what he should do about it, the evangelist replied, "Man, I never would have gotten into it!" That sounds quite brutal, but it does suggest that many of the stressful situations in which we find ourselves could be avoided. Often this is caused by *getting into things which are over our heads.* If your job demands more of you than you can produce, you *will* feel insecure. Consider your situation carefully, and perhaps you will find a way to work that is less demanding. Upon occasion vocational counselors have advised people to do just that. But whatever the cause, we should avoid those circumstances that produce within us a tension which is excessive. This should be no quick decision, however. You might be quite uptight in the early months of a new job and only become relaxed after you've been at it awhile. But if you are still under damaging stress after having been at the same task for a period of years, you might be better off working somewhere else.

Often *being unprepared or untrained produces tenseness.* I know of a young minister who had an attack of nervousness which came upon him suddenly while he was attending a conference. It frightened him because he did not understand it and did not know why it had occurred. Later when he returned home, he very wisely went to his physician. They worked together and looked at his life for clues to his predicament. They decided that his nervousness stemmed from his lack of preparation for the Sunday service. He busied himself so much during the week with calling in the homes of his people, visiting the hospitals, and doing the administrative work of his church that he had little time to prepare his Sunday sermons. As a result he was under constant pressure which kept him tense. The doctor suggested that he reorganize his routine and spend more time on his sermons since this was the most demanding part of his ministry. He did that, and his nervousness disappeared.

It is also true that *some people are tense even in their moments of relaxation.* One reason for this is that many feel guilty while they are playing. They think about things they have left undone and their play is spoiled.

The great Christian psychiatrist Paul Tournier says that a sense of guilt is the seasoning of our daily lives. It gives us an uneasy conscience and prods us to do our work. But it may also keep us from relaxing when we play. Of course, if we go out to play leaving much unfinished work, we are likely to have guilt feelings. In a sense, we should earn the right to play by doing our work well. But this can be overdone. We will never get everything in line just as we would like in our work, and we must have the courage and faith to leave one thing undone in order to do another. Without putting a premium on laziness, we must accept the fact that we are not perfect people, and we should not let ourselves become uptight when we play by feeling guilty.

There is another type of person who gets tense when he plays. He is the competitive individual who takes his competition to the golf course or YMCA. He must succeed there just as he does at his business. So he strains at recreation, even fusses at it, throws a golf club when he misses a shot or sets for himself tough goals for physical fitness at the Y. Such a person will never learn the values of relaxed play until he changes his recreational outlook. He must learn to leave his competitive instincts behind and play for the sheer fun of it.

Also, *a lack of order and discipline in your life may produce tension.* You are bound to be frustrated if you do not manage yourself with some care. Many people do not know how to use their time. Their lives are lived in helter-skelter fashion. No wonder they are tensed up. The antidote to this is to schedule life day by day, doing the most important things first and then the less important, and having some accounting at the end of the day. It is just as important to review your day when it is over as to prepare for its beginning. You will be relaxed if you have planned your work, have carried it out, and can sense this when the day closes. That makes a soft pillow on which to sleep!

To accomplish this, some people think it is helpful to make a list of the things they wish to do each day, checking off the items as they are accomplished. Any plan is a good one as long as this accountability is taken care of. Have you ever noticed the ease with which Jesus moved through every day? Everything seemed to be planned. He knew where he was going and what he hoped to do.

A year or so ago my wife and I went to a football game at Sanford Stadium in Athens, Georgia, where the University of Georgia was playing Pittsburgh in the season's opener. Our seats were high on the second deck. We were too far removed from the players' bench to observe the actions of Georgia Coach Vince Dooley. This didn't affect us very much, however, because three rows back of us we had a coach! From the beginning of the game until the end, a young fellow shouted his admonitions to the Bulldog team. Had Coach Dooley listened to his advice, I am sure that he might have won the game! When the Georgia team took the football on offense, there was one admonition which this fellow repeated again and again: "All right, team, let's be methodical!" Unfortunately, the team did not hear him, and they lost the contest! But our coach did have a point. It is important to put some order in our lives if we are to perform at our best. Self-management gives us direction and poise which frees us from tension.

We would be wise also to *make use of humor*. Humor is the most relaxing mood into which you can enter other than prayer. If, when you begin to tense up, you can learn to laugh at yourself, you will find the tenseness broken. Sometimes it is this attitude which saves our relationships as husbands and wives. Recently a man said about his marriage, "My wife and I have a perfect agreement. I don't try to run her life, and I don't try to run mine!" No doubt this man is relaxed!

A touch of humor can take us through many a strained situation. Bruce Larson, well-known preacher and writer, told a story about a man who received a visitor at his home one day. As the front door was opened, the visitor walked in accompanied by a dog. Nothing was said about the dog as the two men sat down in the living room to converse. In a few moments they both heard the sound of broken glass, and soon the dog appeared in the living room and jumped upon the sofa with his muddy feet. At this the man who lived there said to the visitor, "Don't you think you should have trained your dog better than that?" "My dog?" exclaimed the visitor. "I thought it was your dog!"[1] Here again we see humor as being a great relaxer which adds spice to life. To be able to laugh at situations that involve ourselves is very important.

Another help comes when you *share your life with others*. Here you will need to be selective. It is impossible for you to have many close personal friends during your lifetime. There simply isn't time to cultivate them nor moments enough to enjoy their company. Most of us have a few people in whose presence we feel relaxed. We should cultivate this warm circle and share our lives with those whom we trust. We are more dependent on them than we know. In his mercy and goodness God has given us a kind of comfort that can come only from others.

Another help in reducing tension is to *learn how to relax*. You must relax yourself—body, mind, and spirit. You can learn how to relax your body, if you haven't already mastered this. There are exercises for this purpose which are offered by various groups. A good one is to lie flat on your back and begin deliberately to flex and then relax the muscles of your body from your toes to your head. It takes a few minutes, but it is worth the effort. You can use this technique before dropping off to sleep at night.

To relax your mind, first consciously empty it of any negative feelings. Then think positively about something which relaxes you in nature. Any constructive and peaceful thought will do. Two students in seminary found themselves in an area of America where the winters were bitterly cold. There were many days when they did not see the sun. The skies were heavy and the ground was covered with ice and snow. As a visual relief to those days, the students learned that they could rent cheerful pictures for their dormitory rooms. It helped relax their minds and divert their attention in the midst of cold days. So when you are tense, turn your mind to something that is restful—a lake, a flowing stream, a walk in the woods, soothing music, or something else which interests you.

Many people discover relaxation through diversion. The noted biblical scholar, James Moffatt, is a good example. It is said that the life-style of Dr. Moffatt could be observed by noting three tables which were in his study: On one was a manuscript in progress; on another there was work for a manuscript on Tertullian; on a third was the manuscript of a detective novel he was writing. This noted New Testament scholar found diversion in writing detective stories! Dr. Moffatt was also an avid baseball fan. He taught in America for a while and had an ardent interest in one of the New York baseball teams. He knew the names of all the players, their batting averages, and many personal facts about their lives. It seems strange that such a noted scholar, whose translation of the Bible into modern English was one of the first to break upon the world scene, could give precious time to attending baseball games! No doubt this diversion helped him relax his busy mind.

But beyond all activities, the spirit is best relaxed by *making use of a quiet time.* There are many groups urging this upon us today. They suggest that we plan our day to include two or three periods of fifteen to twenty minutes each to be used for meditation. To some people this sounds new, but actually it is a practice which is quite old. Centuries ago Christian scholars and saints developed what they called choir offices. The words are misleading, for they mean periods of prayer at various intervals during the day within the chancel area of the church. These men knew the power to be found in quiet and prayerful meditation. They knew what is meant to "rest in the Lord, to wait patiently for him." It is still important to take time to draw aside and enter into meditation and prayer. Find yourself some quiet place where the surroundings are congenial to uninterrupted reflection. Let it become a hallowed spot of prayer and devotion.

There are many helpful books for this endeavor. Across the years they have streamed from the presses. The books of Henri Nouwen are among the newest and best. This young Roman Catholic Yale professor is a fresh, new voice leading us again to the altar of prayer and devotion. The books of other years continue to bless us—Thoreau, Underhill, Fosdick, and others.

Such books always help, but more than anything else the Bible speaks to our tension-ridden lives. There are golden verses of Scripture which we can hold in mind and repeat to ourselves often. To live in the constancy of these mighty thoughts, is to know the door that opens into God's presence.

So if tension is your problem, if you are an uptight person, there is something you can do about it. With your best efforts and God's help, you can manage stress that is harmful to your best living.

10

Sometimes It's Good to Be Alone

How gracious, how benign, is Solitude.
—William Wordsworth

In America a phenomenon of the twentieth century has been the rush of people from rural areas to the city. There are many reasons for this, but obviously the main one has been the difference in job opportunities. Also, country life is lonely, and we have a herd instinct that draws us toward the larger group. So we crowd our cities only to discover that the big city gets to us. Its noise and pressures bother us so much that we want the best of two worlds—the city *and* the country. We want to work in the city and live farther and farther away from it. This surely says something about human beings. While you and I want to be a part of the larger group, at times we feel a need to slip away and be alone.

This is much like the experience of Jesus. No doubt he was excited as he moved among the multitudes and was able to meet their needs, but there were times when he wanted to withdraw from them. This leads us to discuss solitude and the obvious truth that some of it is a must for the complete life. Actually, a person who can never bear to be alone, who must always be reinforced by the presence of others, gives evidence of instability. It may be that he lacks personal confidence. Others become his security blanket since he has little security within himself.

Of course, there is another side to this, for you may be crying out in protest, "I'm lonely, what I need is people!" I can understand this and to a point you are quite right. We do need others. Many people must live in enforced loneliness. This is a problem in particular for older people whose isolation leaves them depressed. They desperately need to be associated with others. A person who is always alone may lack reaffirmation of selfhood that others bring, lose all social graces, grow untidy, and make little contribution to the world of which he or she is a part. We find our own self-identity as we become a part of the group. When I shake your hand I am aware of you, and I am also aware of me! I find myself in relationship to you. A recluse fails to discover this and becomes peculiar in his behavior. This is illustrated in a story about the dropping of a nuclear bomb in Appalachia. After the event, a strange fellow dressed in a badly tattered Confederate uniform came out of the Smoky Mountains and said, "I don't know about General Lee, but I'm surrendering!" The recluse needs the world, no doubt about that!

But too much of the group wears us out, leaves us drained, and even momentarily disoriented. We feel as though we've been in a revolving door. One fellow entered an airport, walked up to the information desk and instead of asking for flight information, inquired, "What does it all mean in the grand scheme of things?" Yes, what? After much hustle and bustle, it is only natural to seek brief periods of solitude.

There are many reasons for wanting to be alone. We need solitude often just to get our bearings. We need to get away by ourselves in order to reflect. That is why self-imposed holidays are important. When life seems to be running together, when our goals are not clear, when we lose the zest for living, we need to slip away for some uninterrupted meditation. Usually this does the trick. We return to our daily routine with things again in true focus.

A person should be granted the privilege to suffer alone when he has been hurt. This is almost a law of nature. We know that an animal will crawl into the bushes to lick its wounds when it has been injured. It will even die there alone. This also happens to people. It happened to Jesus. When word reached Jesus that his cousin, John the Baptist, had been beheaded by Herod, he wanted to leave everyone. This was not easy since hungry crowds surrounded him, seeking to be fed. Soon, however, he sent his disciples away so he could be by himself. There he agonized over this painful loss.

Grief is a very personal thing. No one can carry it for us. Friends try, and we are grateful for them, but each of us must work through his own grief. Perhaps it is wise to say, "Let friends be near, but not too near." The pain will be greater without them, but for a little while let the grief process work in solitude. The moment will come when we will return to our friends.

Not only is this true with the loss of a loved one or friend, but with any kind of disappointment that is difficult to take. The greatest preacher in America at the turn of the century was Phillips Brooks; however, he had not always been successful. He first tried teaching and failed. He could not discipline his students, so he left the classroom in embarrassment and what he thought was disgrace. When his friends called about him, his father said, "Phillips will not see anyone now." He was licking his wounds in personal sorrow. But at length, he rose, shook himself like a great lion, and returned to friends and work.

One also has a right to be alone during the creative moments of one's life. Most of the ideas born in this world did not come from committees but from individuals. Committees don't write poems, songs, or prayers as a rule. Such ideas spring from solitude. It is in aloneness that our greatest thoughts seem to come. Take Isaac Newton sitting silently watching an apple fall from a tree or Einstein meditating in a badly cluttered office at Princeton University, thinking great thoughts about the universe—in solitude new ideas often come to us.

It is good, also, to be alone when important decisions are to be made. This marked Jesus' life. He prayed alone before the hard choices of his ministry. He began his public life at the age of thirty. Right off he went to be alone in a garden of prayer. There he had to make decisions about his ministry. Would he take the spectacular route? Would he take shortcuts to success? Every such thought was quickly rejected. He would walk the way of service and love. Later he was to be alone in Gethsemane. The question there was, would he die or live? Should he compromise or would he take the cross? What would the Father have him do? Jesus really suffered through that decision. I think he wanted to live, and everything human in him cried out against an untimely death. Yet after praying in the garden alone, he chose the cross. No matter that three of his disciples slept near by. He needed them, but it was his decision to make.

So, ultimately, decision-making is personal. We confer with friends and confidants and do everything we can to get the best information for the decisions we must make, but we make the choice alone. Think of Beethoven in this regard in Bonn, Germany. The home where he was born and lived is now a museum where, in a poignant exhibit, there is a large glass case filled with strange ear trumpets, all shapes and sizes, from an inch to three feet in length. All were used by Beethoven who went stone deaf and never heard some of his greatest melodies. But Beethoven said, "I will seize fate by the throat. . . . I will hear in heaven." Such words come from those who have won the victory in agonizing solitude.

Aloneness is also a time to keep intact our relationship with God. Not that this is the only place we find him. He confronts us along the path of duty where his presence is unmistakably real. Every minister knows this. He is in the hospital room, the counseling session, and even the committee meeting. But he comes to us most helpfully when we are alone in prayer. There we know him and receive his direction and purpose for our lives.

Such a relationship demands discipline. We must make the time for it, whatever the cost. Charles Darwin, the noted scientist, said that in his younger years he learned to appreciate music, art, and literature. Later he became so caught up in scientific travels and writings that he reached a point where he could not endure to read a line of poetry and found Shakespeare dull. Commenting on this he said, "If I had my life to live over again, I would make it a rule to read some poetry and listen to some music at least once every week just to keep the faculty alive." How similar this is to the Christian's discipline of himself. Neglect is perilous since it produces greater neglect, just as living in untidiness produces a greater mess in a home. One must go to church, for example, to keep alive the ability to worship. That's why doing only what one feels like doing is unwise and even disastrous. The same is true of being alone with God. We may not have the time, but we must find it. As the hymn says, "*Take time* to be holy."

We really possess our souls in being alone. You

see people who are a bit of everything, who do not display any real strength, who are like a weathervane, blowing and turning any way the wind blows. Others seem under control, God-directed, strong, and self-possessed. These are the people we really envy.

In a radio interview, a man from Washington who knows its social life was asked why big parties there never include top movie stars and other celebrities of this type. He answered that it was because Washington puts emphasis not on glamor but on power. That may be true, and in recent years this power has shown a tendency to corrupt. That is why another power—power of soul—becomes so important. It is a strength of person that comes from being near God. It is power in the Holy Spirit. It is charisma born, not of wealth, but of his possession of us. It transcends any earthly attainment which dies with changes in one's earthly fortunes. It can be gained in large measure through prayerful solitude. All of us have known such people, and they have left us the better for it. Consciously or unconsciously we have wanted to be like them, for we know that when the winds really begin to blow they will stand, and that's what it's all about.

So, the sum of all this is take time to be alone. Some may find it strange at first. They've been too long in the revolving door. But there are times and places for solitude and its well-established benefits. As one hymn writer put it in a prayer:

> Mid all the traffic of the ways,
> Turmoils without, within,

SOMETIMES IT'S GOOD TO BE ALONE

Make in my heart a quiet place,
  And come and dwell there-in:

A little shrine of quietness,
  All sacred to thyself,
Where thou shalt all my soul possess,
  And I may find myself.[1]

11

Overcoming Your Fears

Life only demands from you the strength you possess. Only one feat is possible—not to have run away.
　　　　　　　—Dag Hammerskjold, *Markings*

If you were to say that you have never known fear in your life, you would not be taken seriously. At one time or another each of us has been afraid. Every day thousands of people are so overcome by their fears that they are made both miserable and ineffective. Fear can produce a state of paralysis and cause us to suffer defeat in spite of abilities we know we possess.

Ministers often see fear at work while they are officiating at weddings. They know that this is the long-awaited moment for the bride and groom, and that there is bound to be some nervousness. Sometimes a bride or groom will reach such a state of consternation that he or she shakes visibly. Both know the ceremony well because they have rehearsed it, but in spite of this reassurance some couples are still overcome. They find their voices reduced to a whisper, their hands clammy, and a few have collapsed! They know that fear is real. A wedding is only one experience in which fear can be observed. There are many others, so many in fact, that this malady touches the life of everyone.

As a rule some fear is to be expected and is quite normal. It may even be desirable. If the deer did not fear for its life, it could not survive the dangers of the forest. Normal fear is the mother of invention. It has brought forth cures for disease and in many ways has made for personal safety. Fear of disease has led to many helpful discoveries in science and medicine. Fear for your personal safety makes you use caution in crossing the street and prompts you to fasten your seat belt before driving your car. All of this is good. In these cases fear has a positive value.

But fear may get out of hand and do more harm than good. A student should fear failure in his studies; but when this fear becomes so exaggerated that he fails an examination for which he was well prepared, fear has become not a friend but an enemy. A speaker should fear failure before an audience, but he may fear it so much that his mind refuses to function. He may even stutter. Fear of stuttering is one of the reasons why the stutterer stutters!

Perhaps most disconcerting of all are the phobias or irrational fears: fear of closed places, fear of high places, fear of wide open spaces, fear of animals, fear of insects, fear of others, and fear of fear itself. It is said that such an abnormal fear was the cause of Lord Byron's death. As a young man he was told by a gypsy fortuneteller that he would die at age thirty-seven. This made such an impression on him that he never forgot it. When he became ill during his thirty-seventh year, he felt that this was the call of fate. Fear and dread paralyzed his nerve, depleted his energies, and helped bring on his untimely death—so his doctor felt.[1]

You probably get your fears from some source other than a fortuneteller, but you know how real they can be. Dr. W. E. Sangster did not miss the mark when he stated that "more people are suffering from scarecoma than glaucoma, from fearosis than cillosis, from apprehendicitis than appendicitis."[2]

Thus everyone suffering from fear will ask, "How do I handle it?" In attempting to answer this question, let's take a look at a man who knew fear's damaging impact, Saint Paul, the great apostle of Christ. How do we know that Paul had to deal with fear? Because he tells us plainly in his writings. He wrote a letter to some followers who lived in Corinth, where he had preached and a church had been organized. In his letter, he recalls the spirit in which he first visited them. "I was with you in weakness and in much fear and trembling" (I Cor. 2:3). So, even a great man can be afraid.

Paul may have been afraid as a result of a painful defeat in Athens, the hub of Greece. No doubt his spirit was still smarting under this. He had sought to fight out his faith with the Greeks on their own field—that of philosophy—but his sermon on Mars Hill seems not to have impressed his hearers. This may have made him afraid to stand before another hostile audience.

In addition, Paul seems to have possessed few handsome features. He states that his manner of speaking was criticized. He may have been handicapped by faulty vision. We do know that he possessed some "thorn in the flesh." These and other unknown limitations may have made him insecure in his own strength. Whatever the cause, it is obvious that he felt the paralyzing hand of fear. But we know that Paul overcame this condition. He never would have endeared himself to the Christian church as the great apostle if this had not happened.

When we seek a clue to Paul's success, he gives it to us in one of his letters, a pastoral epistle to a young preacher whose name was Timothy. Timothy was fearful and timid, and had a right to be. He lived in Lystra, where Paul had been stoned for his faith. Timothy may have feared this punishment for himself. In addition, he did not appear to be sound of body. But Paul cheered him by these encouraging words: "God hath not give us the spirit of fear; but of power, and of love, and of a sound mind" (II Tim. 1:7 KJ). I believe that all we need to conquer fear is found in these words. With such a way open to us, fear iself may be put to flight. What did Paul mean when he spoke to Timothy of a sound mind? Weymouth's translation of these words is "sound judgment." Another translation is "self-control or sober good sense." The meaning is about the same in each case: *God has given us our common sense to use in facing our fears.* We must keep ourselves reminded of this.

When we use sound judgment, we observe that most of our fears are acquired, a truth which has been demonstrated by scientific experiment. Psychologists tell us that a baby has only two fears, the fear of loud noises and the fear of falling. Dr. John B. Watson discovered this years ago in his celebrated experiments at the Johns Hopkins Maternity Hospital. He took a little boy whose name was Albert and subjected him to all sorts of fearsome experiences. He discovered that the little fellow feared only noise and falling. He did not fear the dark, nor a bucket of flaming newspapers, nor the animals that older children feared. To prove that a baby has no fear of animals, he took Albert to the zoo and held him close to every animal. The only time he showed any emotion whatsoever was when a camel breathed in his face. As one author put it, a camel's breath is not exactly attar of roses!

Dr. Watson then proceded to prove that Albert could learn to fear. In his experiments, Dr. Watson paired the striking of a steel bar, which created such a noise that Albert cried when this was done, with a white rat. The bar was struck just as the white rat was dropped into Albert's crib. When the baby cried, the rat was removed, and he was given other toys. When Albert was again happy, the bar was struck again and the rat returned to the crib. Again Albert cried. After ten repetitions, Albert would cry when the rat was dropped into his crib, even though the bar had not been struck. Albert, by fear association, had learned to fear something that was no threat to his comfort at all. In addition, it was discovered that he feared other things that had any of the features of the white rat. A toy that scampered across the room made him cry. Other furry animals displeased him. A ball of fur, a Santa Claus mask, a fur coat—all frightened him. He associated these with the rat he had come to fear.[3] What this says to us is plain. We learn most of our fears. We may learn them from our parents. You may be fear-ridden because your parents were that way.

One morning as a family ate breakfast, husband and wife were expressing their fears about the welfare of a friend. They realized how unwise this was when their five-year-old said, "Daddy, you must be afraid of everything!" Already the child was learning fear, and while her parents would want her to fear some things, they would not want her whole world to become one of fright. They were knowledgeable people and tried to be wiser after that experience at the breakfast table.

Most of our fears develop out of threats to our security. We may feel that we will lose our lives, our health, our jobs, our faith, our loved ones, or our social acceptance. It is to such fears that we must apply our best thinking. We must face up to them and see them for what they are.

Good sense tells us that we will probably want to run from our fears or fight them. In either case, they will defeat us. When I was in theological seminary, I found myself confronted with certain theological views which were a challenge to all I had come to believe. Naturally I was disturbed and frightened. I found myself tempted to change seminaries, but deep within I knew that if I fled the scene I could never respect myself as I should. I knew, too, that I would then always carry this fear with me. So I did not run. I stayed on and fought instead. Again I found myself being defeated. I continued to be insecure and afraid. It was not until I ceased running and fighting and began to face this fear that I won the victory over it. It was not easy, but in the end I developed a stronger theology than I had before. During this experience I learned a lesson I have never forgotten. When confronting something of which we are afraid, it is futile to fight or flee. We must face such things as calmly as we can. When we do, we will discover that there is little cause to be afraid.

Two friends were in Brussels in 1958 on the day all of Belgium celebrated its independence. They were at the World Exhibition grounds waiting with thousands for certain festivities to begin in which the king would participate. Suddenly in the distance they saw what appeared to be a huge man fifteen or more feet in height. His very presence seemed to be disturbing the little children no end. But as the two got nearer to him, they discovered that he was only a little man on stilts.

This is the way with fear. Often it is magnified out of all proportion. We need only face it with a sound mind and self-control, and analyze it for what it is to discover that it will often dwindle before our very eyes. God says to us, therefore, "I have given you a sound mind. Use it! Face up to your fears!"

But Paul has another word for us. The word is love. "To control your fears, God has given you love," wrote Paul. John said the same thing when he wrote, "Perfect love casts out fear."

There can be no doubt about the truth of this. Love for others or for some cause greater than self makes us bold. This was part of Paul's secret. He was not naturally courageous, but because he loved someone else more than himself he displayed splendid courage. John Knox, the great leader in the Protestant Reformation, shook with fear upon occasion, but he loved the truth and right so much that his fears were overcome. As he was lowered into his grave, it was said of him: "Here was one who feared God so much that he never feared the face of man." This might have been said of Luther and Wesley also.

Sometimes love makes a person so bold that he gladly gives his life for another. That is especially true of parents and children. A father gives a kidney to a son—that has happened many times. I know of an instance in which a mother ran to snatch her errant little one from the path of an oncoming train only to be killed along with the child. That was a terrible accident, but the mother gave her life because she loved. Love made her brave in the face of fear. All of this indicates why loving is so important.

Paul's final word for us is power. God gave us power with which we can face our fears.

Charles Allen tells a story of a lonely woman living in a big city who used to call a number each night to get the correct time. Someone asked her if she had a clock. She answered, "Yes. I call not because I want to know the time but to hear somebody's voice before I go to bed." A human voice is often comforting but never so much as the Divine voice. How many times have we been lonely and afraid only to hear God's voice! Certainly Paul, fighting God's battles at some lonely outpost, heard that voice again and again. He had fears, but God delivered him from them all. That was his constant testimony.

The best antidote for fear is faith. When we fear for tomorrow, have fears about our health or about some loved one; when terrible and irrational fears descend upon us; when we fear for our success, our place in the sun; or when we have so many fears that we are frightened of fear itself; the word that must be in our hearts is faith. We must believe enough to take hold of God.

There is an intimate story which points to this truth told by the Scottish Evangelist, John McNeill. As a lad he worked at an out-of-the way railroad station. On Saturday nights he often walked home to spend Sunday with his parents. It was a fearful ordeal, done late at night after the office had closed. The road along which he had to walk was dark and lonely. At times he found himself afraid. One night as he made his way home it seemed darker than usual. Suddenly he heard footsteps approaching. They almost paralyzed him with fright. Then came a familiar voice: "Is that you, John?" It was the voice of his father who, knowing the darkness of the night, had come to walk home with him. John McNeill said about that experience: "I just slipped my hand in his and was no longer afraid of anything."

The act of faith is open to us all. With Him holding us, fear itself is frightened away. Faith has put us in the center of his love and care. There we need not fear anything.

12

Be Sure
to Smell the Flowers

And 'tis my faith, that every flower
Enjoys the air it breathes.
—William Wordsworth

The noted golfer Walter Hagen is reported to have said, "Don't hurry and don't worry. You are only here on a short visit, so be sure to smell the flowers." Whoever first said them, these words are appropriate for our time.

Of course there are people who are impatient with such advice. They will argue that the condition of the world dictates that we must hurry and worry. "Forget the flowers," they will say, "involve yourself in the plight of man." It is true that this advice may need to be given to some. Halford Luccock reminded us that Jesus did not say, "If any man would come after me, let him reduce his high blood pressure; but let him take up his cross and follow me." It is such a thought that causes some to argue that no one should seek a slow and carefree life when conditions in the world demand from us a commitment to service.

But keep in mind that the Jesus who spoke of cross-bearing also said: "Be not anxious." "Take no thought for tomorrow." "My peace I give unto you." We are on safe ground, therefore, when we go to

God and seek an answer for our personal needs. Nor is there anything wrong with wanting to smell the flowers! God intended for man to enjoy this life within the pattern of his will. So, while we can agree with those who feel that we should suffer for the world's sake, we hope that they will want to accept the other side of Christ's offering to us.

With this in mind, let us look first at haste and then at worry. These are two enemies to personal peace. Haste confuses and impedes progress. When you are in a hurry, you get in your own way and will often end up running by things without seeing them. Like the man and his wife who were tourists in Europe. He was an art lover, and they were in a well-known museum. He wanted to pause for a moment and study a painting, but the touring group apparently did not have time for this. His wife said to him, "Come on, honey, if you stop to look at something, we won't get to see anything!" It is such haste that keeps us from reaping the harvest of the quiet eye.

Bishop Gerald Kennedy wrote about a man in Kentucky who had a hound with incredible speed. The hound was also a pacifist. He would run right by a fox, having no desire to attack or kill anything. The man reported that it was some experience to see the consternation of the fox when he found himself chasing the hound! All too many of us are like this creature in that we rush through life at such a pace that we run by important things.

Haste keeps us keyed up, reduces our effectiveness, and may give us high blood pressure, among other things. We know from experience that haste impedes any task we are trying to accomplish. We work ourselves into a needless lather when we hurry and find our efficiency going down. Try this on a typewriter sometime: rush the job at hand and everything seems to go wrong. The keys stick, the wrong letters are struck, and misspelling is frequent. Speed is good only to the point that it is free from error. Beyond that it reaches a point of diminishing returns. This does not count the rise in stress and blood pressure under such conditions.

Perhaps it is the frantic pace which contributes to our insomnia. Many people must take sleeping pills at night to ease them down from the day's tensions. If they do not, they lie awake and toss fitfully trying to go to sleep. Here, one can appreciate the humor in one of Dan Tobin's cartoons, *The Little Woman.* The wife Emily is saying to her husband who is trying desperately to go to sleep, "No wonder you can't sleep, lying there with your eyes open all night!" The logic here is confusing, but we can sympathize with the man's plight! Perhaps he was keyed up.

Haste turns life into a hiss or a blur. Things run together, and we do not see them clearly. This helps us to understand one heart attack victim's philosophy of life. It had been his custom to ride to work each day, but after his attack his physician prescribed that he walk to his office. To his delight, he discovered an entirely new world. The slow pace of walking allowed him to see flowers and meet people he would not have met otherwise. The lesson is plain. There are no flowers to smell in this world if you are in too big a hurry!

Worry, another enemy to personal contentment, when combined with haste and indulgence, creates many of our illnesses. And though Jesus said to us, "Be not anxious," we find this hard to achieve. We fume and fidget and get ourselves very much frustrated. We keep asking, among other things, "How am I doing?" "What does the boss think of me?" "What about my health?" We also worry about dying. As we grow older our friends start dropping out, and we wonder when it will happen to us. Actually, this concern begins quite young. In that delightful book, *Children's Letters to God*, one little boy writes, "Dear God, what is it like when you die? Nobody will tell me. I just want to know, I don't want to do it. Your friend Mike."[1] We can certainly understand these sentiments, for they are our own.

The antidote to such a combination of worry and fear is faith. When we believe strongly enough in God, we are freed from such nagging concerns and living slows down to an unhurried pace. Then it is that we have time for the flowers! But we must ask now, "What flowers are there to smell?" We readily observe that human experience is prolific. We cannot hope to mention every delight, but there are some we should not miss.

We should certainly inhale the sweet aromas that arise from meaningful work. Nothing is more important to our peace of mind than the work we do, and Christianity has always been interested in a proper interpretation of vocation. Some people think that Christianity means the Sabbath experience in the sanctuary and that the good news has no word for the marketplace. They are wrong. God has something to say about our jobs.

The boredom experienced among workers today is appalling. All the psycho-cybernetics and personnel wizardry of the day do not seem to be able to convince us otherwise, though we keep trying. An article by Chris Argyris entitled "We Must Make Work Worthwhile" appeared in *Life* magazine. In the article the author indicated that he had spoken with both industrial theorists and workers. The theorists seemed to feel that employers could win by persuading employees that their jobs were important. Their conversation usually ran like this: "Even though yours is a small part of a big product, don't you see that if you didn't put in your bolts correctly, the whole product would be ruined. You are important!" However well-intended these words were, there was an indication that they only upset workers the more. As one worker told the writer, "How would you like to get up in the morning, look at yourself in the mirror and say to yourself, 'The most important thing I can do is place four bolts in the rear end of a car'?" Argyris answered the question by asking another, "But what would you want management to do? Tell you that it is a dull, boring, and uninteresting job?" With this the worker's eyes lighted up. "If they did, it would be the first time in eight years they weren't lying."[2] That's pretty hard stuff, isn't it?

Perhaps it is wise to begin any discussion of jobs

with an admission that there is a certain amount of boredom in any undertaking. Honesty dictates this. This does not mean that people should never change their jobs. We might be fit for one task and unfit for another. Boredom may be reduced as we come closer to doing the thing for which we have gifts and interest. But we should never expect to eliminate boredom entirely.

Beyond all of this, we should still understand that work is our salvation. It puts tone in our spirits and adds meaning to our lives. We sense this from the results of a recent advertisement which appeared in *The New York Times.* Part-time work was offered to whoever might apply. Hundreds of applications were received from retired men, indicating that everyone likes to have something to do. I know a man who grew nervous in his retirement and was ordered back to work by his physician. Usually it is the opposite condition which prevails. A man grows nervous in his work, and it is suggested that he retire. In this one case, however, work seemed to be the answer to a personal need. Now that the mandatory retirement age for American workers has been raised from sixty-five to seventy, the benefits of work can be received much longer. This will be a blessing for many persons.

Meaning may be found if we see our work as a contribution to life. One man was both railroad agent and telegrapher in a small town. A representative from a children's home visited his office one day, leaving the agent greatly impressed. When the visitor left, he said to a friend standing nearby, "I wish I had the job that man's got. All I do around here is pound brass and draw monthly pay checks." How wrong he was! A little imagination would have allowed him to see that through his fingers there flowed daily messages to other human beings of love, warning, tragedy, and hope. He was a channel for the very stuff of life had he been willing to see it. How different is a shoe repairman whom I know. With a bright glow on his face he says, "I am a shoe repairman. All God's chillun gotta have shoes, and I intend to keep them repaired!" This humble man has found meaning in his work because he sees it to be an honorable vocation and a service which he can render to others. It is only when our work is seen in this light that we are able to enjoy it most. Then we smell the flowers.

Also, be sure to inhale the fragrance of friendship. To have friends is a blessed thing indeed. As someone has said, "A man is only half of himself; his friends are the other half." For this reason we should make every effort to establish friendships which benefit others and ourselves.

Of course, we must understand the true meaning of this relationship. Friends, if they are strong ones, help us a great deal. Perhaps this is what prompted Elizabeth Barrett Browning to write Charles Kingsley to ask, "What, Sir, is the secret of your life? Tell me, that I may make mine beautiful, too." "Madam," Kingsley replied, "I had a friend." It was of such a relationship that Jesus spoke when he said to his disciples, "I have called you my friends."

I would like to add my own testimony here. When

I was a student at Emory University, my fraternity urged me during my junior year to run for a campus office. After some persuasion, I finally agreed to enter into what was my first and only venture in politics. When it was announced that I would be in the race, many of my friends sought me out and offered their support. But this was not true of one of my closest friends. One day we met on the campus, and he told me that although he appreciated me, he could not vote for me in the election. He insisted that I already had enough extracurricular duties and any additional campus responsibility would interfere with my studies. This shocked me so much that I can still remember the spot where we met, though it has been many years. When a runoff election was held, I lost the race by about one hundred votes. During the months that followed, I thought often of those words spoken to me by that good friend who would not support me. I came to realize the wisdom of what he had said. It would not have been wise for me to undertake anything more. Today we are still the closest of friends, and he still tells me when he thinks I am wrong! He also wants me to be his friend in the same manner. That's the only basis upon which true friendship can be established. It means that each really cares.

Married life needs this same element of friendship. It has been said that "Life is just one thing after another, and love is two fool things after each other!" While romantic love is wonderful, it may fail unless deeper ties are established. That is why many lovers are also genuine companions and friends. One is twice blessed if one likes the person one loves.

Be aware of a love for others that serves. This is a scented flower no one can afford to miss. It is a certain guarantee for fulfillment. Bel Kaufmann reveals this truth in her delightful book *Up the Down Staircase.* She is a teacher in a slum school where many of her students are problem children, some with court records. She is often tempted to resign and go to a better school, but she stays because she sees what good can happen to the children. In one instance she recounts her attempt to make law, order, and government become real for the children in her class. She announced one day that on the following day the classroom would be turned into a courtroom and that a trial would take place. She then proceeded to appoint students to the various positions necessary for the trial. As judge, she selected a little boy whose name was José Rodriquez. When she mentioned his name there were snickers among the children, but she stuck to her choice. The next day José appeared in black gown and mortar board with a heavy hammer for his gavel. He bore the gavel with such solemn dignity that no one dared rise. José, living his role to the hilt, said, "The court clerk is supposed to say they gotta' rise." One by one the class rose, and the judge ordered the session to begin. Judge José overruled every objection from the lawyers. He said, "Maybe I'm stupid, but I'm the judge and you gotta' listen." When a brash young fellow named Harry Kagan, who had been appointed as a lawyer, challenged him on court procedure, José drew on his past experience of delinquency and said, "I ought to know. I been." When the bell rang, Miss Kaufmann reported that José slowly removed his cap and gown, folded them neatly over his notebook, and went on to his next class. But she added that he walked as if he were still vested in his judicial robe! "I don't think he will ever be the same again," she said. With this she added her own postscript: "And . . . that's why I want to teach; that's the one and only compensation; to make a permanent difference in the life of a child."[3] Surely in that moment the sweet fragrance of love was hers.

Such a rewarding life is possible for each of us if we have the will to pursue it. It is there for our enjoyment if we learn to walk slowly, think positively, inhale deeply, believe fervently, and love generously. Do these things and you will not miss the wonderful thing this life was meant to be.

2. Henry David Thoreau, *Walden* (New York: W. W. Norton, 1951), p. 343.

3. Elton Trueblood, *The New Man for Our Time* (New York: Harper & Row, 1970), p. 121.

Chapter 7: Dealing with Grief

1. Erich Segal, *Love Story* (New York: Harper & Row, 1970), p. 130.

2. J. Carter Swaim, *Body, Soul, and Spirit* (New York: Thomas Nelson, 1957), p. 205.

3. C. S. Lewis, *Letters to an American Lady* (Grand Rapids, Michigan: W. B. Eerdmans, 1967), p. 89.

4. John Henry Newman, "Lead, Kindly Light," *The Book of Hymns* (Nashville, Tennessee: The United Methodist Publishing House, 1966), No. 272.

Chapter 8: Don't Lose Heart

1. Edward Everett Hale, *The Treasury of Religious Verse,* comp. Donald T. Kauffman (Old Tappan, N.J.: Fleming H. Revell, 1952), p. 236.

2. J. Wallace Hamilton, *Horns and Halos* (Old Tappan, N.J.: Fleming H. Revell, 1954), p. 93.

Chapter 9: Living with Tension

1. Bruce Larson, *The One and Only You* (Waco, Texas: Word Books, 1974), p. 98.

Chapter 10: Sometimes It's Good to Be Alone

1. John Oxenham, "Mid All the Traffic of the Ways," *The Book of Hymns* (Nashville: The United Methodist Publishing House, 1966), No. 225.

Chapter 11: Overcoming Your Fears

1. Carl Wallace Petty, *The Evening Altar* (Nashville: Abingdon-Cokesbury, 1940), p. 63.

2. W. E. Sangster, *The Secret of Radiant Life* (Nashville: Abingdon Press, 1957), p. 212.

3. Matthew N. Chappell, *In the Name of Common Sense* (New York: Macmillan Company, 1943), pp. 75-77.

Chapter 12: Be Sure to Smell the Flowers

1. Eric Marshall and Stuart Hample, *Children's Letters to God* (New York: An Essendess Special Edition, 1967).

2. Chris Argyris, "We Must Make Work Worthwhile," *Life* (May 5, 1967).

3. Bel Kaufman, *Up the Down Staircase* (Englewood Cliffs, N.J.: Prentice-Hall, 1964), p. 137.

NOTES

Chapter 1: Be Good to Yourself

1. Mildred Newman and Bernard Berkowitz, *How to Be Your Own Best Friend* (New York: Ballantine Books, 1971), p. 25.
2. Alvin Toffler, *Future Shock* (New York: Bantam Books, 1971), pp. 378-79.

Chapter 2: Big Worries and God's Care

1. W. H. Lewis, *Letters of C. S. Lewis* (New York: Harcourt, Brace and World, 1966), p. 306.
2. Toyohiko Kagawa, *The Challenge of Redemptive Love* (New York: Abingdon Press, 1940), p. 79.

Chapter 3: You and Your Feelings

1. Vincent P. Collins, *Me, Myself, and You* (St. Meinrad, Indiana: Abbey Press, 1976), pp. 52-54.

Chapter 4: Your Personal Health and Peace

1. Paul Tournier, *The Healing of Persons* (New York: Harper & Row, 1965), p. 225.
2. John Wesley, *The Journal of John Wesley* (London: Epworth Press, 1938. Ed. Nehemiah Curnock), Vol. I, p. 478.

Chapter 5: Your Security Blanket

1. Robert L. Short, *The Gospel According to Peanuts* (Richmond: John Knox Press, 1964), p. 104.
2. Ibid., pp. 63-64.
3. Ibid., p. 70.
4. Collins, *Me, Myself, and You*, p. ii.

Chapter 6: Keep on Walking

1. Bruce Larson, *Setting Men Free* (Grand Rapids, Michigan: Zondervan, 1967), p. 33.